# AUGUSTINE:
## A GUIDE FOR THE PERPLEXED

**Continuum Guides for the Perplexed**

Continuum's Guides for the Perplexed are clear, concise and accessible introductions to thinkers, writers and subjects that students and readers can find especially challenging. Concentrating specifically on what it is that makes the subject difficult to grasp, these books explain and explore key themes and ideas, guiding the reader towards a thorough understanding of demanding material.

*Guides for the Perplexed* available from Continuum:
*Adorno: A Guide for the Perplexed*, Alex Thomson
*Arendt: A Guide for the Perplexed*, Karin Fry
*Aristotle: A Guide for the Perplexed*, John Vella
*Bentham: A Guide for the Perplexed*, Philip Schofield
*Berkley: A Guide for the Perplexed*, Talia Bettcher
*Deleuze: A Guide for the Perplexed*, Claire Colebrook
*Derrida: A Guide for the Perplexed*, Julian Wolfreys
*Descartes: A Guide for the Perplexed*, Justin Skirry
*The Empiricists: A Guide for the Perplexed*, Laurence Carlin
*Existentialism: A Guide for the Perplexed,* Stephen Earnshaw
*Freud: A Guide for the Perplexed*, Celine Surprenant
*Gadamer: A Guide for the Perplexed*, Chris Lawn
*Habermas: A Guide for the Perplexed*, Lasse Thomassen
*Hegel: A Guide for the Perplexed*, David James
*Heidegger: A Guide for the Perplexed*, David Cerbone
*Hobbes: A Guide for the Perplexed*, Stephen J. Finn
*Hume: A Guide for the Perplexed*, Angela Coventry
*Husserl: A Guide for the Perplexed*, Matheson Russell
*Kant: A Guide for the Perplexed*, T. K. Seung
*Kierkegaard: A Guide for the Perplexed*, Clare Carlisle
*Leibniz: A Guide for the Perplexed*, Franklin Perkins
*Levinas: A Guide for the Perplexed*, B. C. Hutchens
*Locke: A Guide for the Perplexed*, Patricia Sheridan
*Merleau-Ponty: A Guide for the Perplexed*, Eric Matthews
*Nietzsche: A Guide for the Perplexed*, R. Kevin Hill
*Plato: A Guide for the Perplexed*, Gerald A. Press
*Pragmatism: A Guide for the Perplexed*, Robert B. Talisse and Scott F. Aikin
*Quine: A Guide for the Perplexed*, Gary Kemp
*Relativism: A Guide for the Perplexed*, Timothy Mosteller
*Ricoeur: A Guide for the Perplexed*, David Pellauer
*Rousseau: A Guide for the Perplexed*, Matthew Simpson
*Sartre: A Guide for the Perplexed*, Gary Cox
*Socrates: A Guide for the Perplexed*, Sara Ahbel-Rappe
*Spinoza: A Guide for the Perplexed*, Charles Jarrett
*The Stoics: A Guide for the Perplexed*, M. Andrew Holowchak
*Utilitarianism: A Guide for the Perplexed*, Krister Bykvist
*Wittgenstein: A Guide for the Perplexed*, Mark Addis

# AUGUSTINE:
# A GUIDE FOR THE PERPLEXED

## JAMES WETZEL

Continuum International Publishing Group
The Tower Building    80 Maiden Lane
11 York Road          Suite 704
London SE1 7NX        New York NY 10038

www.continuumbooks.com

© James Wetzel 2010

All rights reserved. No part of this publication may be reproduced or transmitted in any form or by any means, electronic or mechanical, including photocopying, recording, or any information storage or retrieval system, without prior permission in writing from the publishers.

**British Library Cataloguing-in-Publication Data**
A catalogue record for this book is available from the British Library.

ISBN:   HB: 978-1-8470-6195-9
        PB: 978-1-8470-6196-6

**Library of Congress Cataloging-in-Publication Data**
Wetzel, James.
Augustine : a guide for the perplexed / James Wetzel.
p. cm.
Includes bibliographical references (p. ) and index.
ISBN 978-1-84706-195-9 – ISBN 978-1-84706-196-6
1. Augustine, Saint, Bishop of Hippo. I. Title.
B655.Z7W468 2010
189'.2–dc22

2009044688

Excerpt from Rilke's "Turning-Point," trans. William H. Gass, in *Reading Rilke: Reflections on the Problems of Translation*, copyright 1999 by William H. Gass; reprinted by permission of Basic Books, a member of the Perseus Books Group.

Fragment 43, in *Fragments: The Collected Wisdom of Heraclitus*, trans. Brooks Haxton and copyright 2001 by Brooks Haxton; reprinted by permission of Viking Penguin, a division of Penguin Group (USA) Inc.

Excerpt from "The Dry Salvages" in *Four Quartets*, copyright 1941 by T. S. Eliot and renewed 1969 by Esme Valerie Eliot; reprinted by permission of Houghton Mifflin Harcourt Publishing Company.

Typeset by Newgen Imaging Systems Pvt Ltd, Chennai, India

**To the memory of**
Father Thomas Frank Martin, O. S. A. (1943–2009),
lover of Augustine.

Pondus meum amor meus; eo feror, quocumque feror.
*Conf.* 13.9.10

[My weight, my love; I will be borne by it, wherever
I will be borne.]

# CONTENTS

| | |
|---|---|
| *Acknowledgments* | ix |
| *Abbreviations of Works Cited* | x |
| *Note on Translations* | xiv |
| *Figures Invoked* | xv |

| | |
|---|---|
| Prologue: A Life Confessed | 1 |
| Chapter One: Death and the Delineation of Soul | 11 |
|   Virtue Comes to Grief | 17 |
|     Ciceronian plot | 17 |
|     Augustinian dénouement | 21 |
|   The Materialization of Loss | 30 |
|     Trappings of woe | 30 |
|     A grievable God | 38 |
| Chapter Two: Sin and the Invention of Will | 44 |
|   Pathos of Will | 52 |
|     Place of unlikeness | 52 |
|     Debriefing on beauty | 60 |
|   Beauty Memorialized | 63 |
|     From Plato to Paul | 63 |
|     The emotion of time | 70 |
| Chapter Three: Sex and the Infancy of Desire | 77 |
|   The Mythology of Sin | 83 |
|     Grace and original guilt | 83 |
|     Adam, Eve, and the angels | 87 |

## CONTENTS

| | |
|---|---|
| Conversion | 95 |
|     The tie that unbinds | 95 |
|     Learning a first logos | 105 |
| Almost an Epilogue: Time Troubled | 113 |
| *Suggestions Readings Chapter by Chapter* | 127 |
| *General Suggestions for Further Reading* | 136 |
| *Index* | 141 |

# ACKNOWLEDGMENTS

Augustine was never without friends; they reminded him both of the limitation of words and of their great promise. I owe a similar debt of memory to my friends. I want to thank John Bowlin, Michel Barnes, Kathleen Skerrett, Joshua Ramey, and Amisha Patel for reading portions of my typescript and lending me their insights. Eric Gregory, Chuck Mathewes, Jesse Couenhoven, Jonathan Yates, Stanley Hauerwas, Coleman Brown, Anne Ashbaugh, David Burrell, and John Cavadini have for years been gently inspiring my engagement with Augustine. I also want to acknowledge what a boon it has been for me to work at Villanova with Augustinian priests and educators: the late Tom Martin, Marty Laird, Allan Fitzgerald, Danny Doyle, Barbara Wall, and Peter Donohue, to name a few.

Finally I want to thank my family for giving me the time to write this book. Faced the choice of picking up with Augustine or picking up my infant son, Rowan, I sometimes went with Augustine. Of course I could not expect my son to understand. I am not sure that I do. But my wife, Nathalie, helped me to live with my choice and graciously picked up where I left off. I end with a special word of thanks to my daughter, Anna, who paid me the undeserved grace of missing me most of all.

Feast Day of St. Augustine, 2009

# ABBREVIATIONS OF WORKS CITED

## AUGUSTINE

[abbreviation   Latin title, edition, translated title, date of composition]

*an. et or.*   *De anima et eius origine*, CSEL 60, *On the Soul and its Origin* (419/420)
*b. conjug.*   *De bono conjugali*, CSEL 41, *On the Good of Marriage* (401)
*c. Acad.*   *Contra Academicos*, CCL 29, *Against the Skeptics* (386/387)
*c. ep. Pel.*   *Contra duas epistulas Pelagianorum*, CSEL 60, *Against Two Letters of the Pelagians* (421)
*civ. Dei*   *De civitate Dei*, CCL 47–48, *City of God* (413/427)
*c. Jul.*   *Contra Julianum*, PL 44, *Against Julian* (421/422)
*c. Jul. imp.*   *Contra Julianum opus imperfectum*, CSEL 85, *Against Julian*, the unfinished sequel (429/430)
*conf.*   *Confessiones*, O'Donnell, *Confessions* (397/401)
*corrept.*   *De correptione et gratia*, BA 24, *On Admonition and Grace* (426/427)
*doc. Chr.*   *De doctrina Christiana*, CCL 32, *On Christian Doctrine* (396; 426/427)
*duab. an.*   *De duabus animabus*, CSEL 25, *On Two Souls* (392/393)
*ep. 93*   *Epistula ad Vincentium*, CSEL 34.2, *Letter to Vincent, Bishop of Cartenna* (408)
*ex. prop. Rm.*   *Expositio quarundam propositionum ex epistula Apostoli ad Romanos*, CSEL 84, *Commentary on Romans—Selected Verses* (394/395)

x

## ABBREVIATIONS OF WORKS CITED

*Gn. adv. Man.*   *De Genesi adversus Manicheos*, CSEL 91, *On Genesis—the Anti-Manichean Commentary* (388/389)
*Gn. litt.*   *De Genesi ad litteram*, BA 49–50, *On Genesis—the Literal Commentary* (401/415)
*gr. et pecc. or.*   *De gratia Christi et de peccati originali*, CSEL 42, *On the Grace of Christ and Original Sin* (418)
*imm. an.*   *De immortalitate animae*, CSEL 89, *On the Soul's Immortality* (387)
*lib. arb.*   *De libero arbitrio*, CCL 29, *On Free Will* (387/388; 395)
*mag.*   *De magistro*, CCL 29, *On the Teacher* (389)
*mend.*   *De mendacio*, CSEL 41, *On Lying* (394/395)
*nupt. et conc.*   *De nuptiis et concupiscentia*, CSEL 42, *On Marriage and Sexual Desire* (419/421)
*pecc. mer.*   *De peccatorum meritis et remissione et de baptismo parvulorum*, CSEL 60, *On the Merits and Forgiveness of Sins, On Infant Baptism* (411)
*persev.*   *De dono perseverantiae*, BA 24, *On the Gift of Perseverance* (428/429)
*praed. sanct.*   *De praedestinatione sanctorum*, BA 24, *On the Predestination of the Saints* (428/429)
*retr.*   *Retractationes*, CCL 57, *Reconsiderations* (426/427)
*Simpl.*   *Ad Simplicianum*, CCL 44, *To Simplician* (396/398)
*sol.*   *Soliloquia*, CSEL 89, *Soliloquies* (386/387)
*spir. et litt.*   *De spiritu et littera*, CSEL 60, *On the Spirit and the Letter* (412)
*Trin.*   *De Trinitate*, CCL 50–50A, *The Trinity* (399–422/426)
*util. cred.*   *De utilitate credendi*, CSEL 25.1, *On the Advantage of Believing* (391/392)
*vera rel.*   *De vera religione*, CCL 32, *On True Religion* (390–391)
*virg.*   *De sancta virginitate*, CSEL 41, *On Holy Virginity* (401)

For further clarification of the chronology of Augustine's works, see *Augustine Through the Ages: An Encyclopedia*, ed. Allan D. Fitzgerald, O. S. A. (Grand Rapids, MI: Eerdmans, 1999), xlii–il, pp. 299–305, pp. 774–789, and Pierre-Marie Hombert, *Nouvelles recherches de chronologie augustinienne* (Paris: Institut d'Études Augustiniennes, 2000).

## ABBREVIATIONS OF WORKS CITED

## LATIN EDITIONS

| | |
|---|---|
| BA | *Bibliothèque Augustinienne* (Paris: Institut D'Études Augustiniennes) |
| CCL | *Corpus Christianorum Series Latina* (Turnholt: Brepols) |
| CSEL | *Corpus Scriptorum Ecclesiasticorum Latinorum* (Vienna: Hoelder-Pichler-Tempsky) |
| O'Donnell | James J. O'Donnell, *Confessions*, text and commentary (Oxford: Clarendon, 1992) |
| PL | *Patrologia Latina* (Migne) |

## OTHER ANCIENTS

| | |
|---|---|
| *Aen.* | *Aeneid* (Virgil) 29–19 B.C.E. |
| *enn.* | *Enneads* (Plotinus) 253–270; compiled and edited by Porphyry sometime between 301 and 305 |
| *ep. 267* | *Epistula ad Atticum, Letter to his friend Atticus* (Cicero) March 45 B.C.E. |
| *fin.* | *De finibus bonorum et malorum, The Ends of Things Good and Bad* (Cicero) 45 B.C.E. |
| *Tusc.* | *Tusculanae Disputationes, Tusculan Disputations* (Cicero) 45 B.C.E. |

For the Latin text of the *Aeneid*, see *P. Vergili Maronis Opera*, ed. R. A. B. Mynors (Oxford: Clarendon Press, 1969). For the Greek text of the *Enneads*, see the Loeb edition, seven volumes, ed. and trans. A. H. Armstrong, 2nd Edition (Cambridge, MA: Harvard, 1989). For Cicero's Latin, see *De Finibus*, ed. and trans. H. Rackham (Harvard, 1983), *Tusculan Disputations*, ed. and trans. J. E. King (Harvard, 1966), and *Letters to Atticus*, ed. and trans. D. R. Shackleton Bailey (Harvard, 1999)—volumes 17, 18, and 24.3, respectively, of the Loeb Cicero.

## BIBLICAL TEXTS

| | |
|---|---|
| 1 Cor. | Paul's First Letter to the Corinthians |
| Gen. | Genesis |
| Exod. | Exodus |

**ABBREVIATIONS OF WORKS CITED**

| | |
|---|---|
| Jn. | Gospel of John |
| 1 Jn. | The First Letter of John |
| Lk. | Gospel of Luke |
| Matt. | Gospel of Matthew |
| Ps. | The Psalms |
| Rom. | Paul's Letter to the Romans |
| 1 Tim. | Paul's First Letter to Timothy |

# NOTE ON TRANSLATIONS

All the translations of Augustine and the few of Cicero are my own. For Virgil's poetry and the clipped Greek of Plotinus, it seemed wise to lean on others. I turned to Stanley Lombardo for his resonant translation of the *Aeneid* (Indianapolis: Hackett, 2005) and to Stephen MacKenna for his august, early-twentieth century translation of the *Enneads* (New York: Penguin, 1991).

When quoting Genesis, I used Robert Alter's translation of the Hebrew (Berkeley: University of California Press, 1996) when not translating directly from Augustine's Latin. (The choice depended on whether I was making a point about Genesis or a point about Augustine's take on Genesis.)

For those of you looking for a good translation of Augustine's *Confessions*, the choices abound. Here is a handful:

Gary Wills (New York: Penguin, 2006): inventive, at times insouciant, but all-in-all a work of art.

F. J. Sheed (Indianapolis: Hackett, 1993, a reissue): the translation favored by Peter Brown, Augustine's best biographer; each book is prefaced by a summary outline.

Henry Chadwick (New York: Oxford University Press, 1991): not very literary, but dependable; the scholar's choice for the classroom.

Maria Boulding (Brooklyn: New City Press, 1997): perhaps the best combination of literary sensitivity and scholarly restraint.

# FIGURES INVOKED

Ambrose (339–397): celebrated rhetor turned bishop; appointed to the See of Milan in 374; his sermons in the mid 380s alert Augustine to allegorical readings of the Old Testament and to Platonist conceptions of divine substance; baptizes Augustine in Milan, Easter of 387.

Antiochus of Ascalon (c. 130–68 B.C.E.): first studies at Plato's Academy under the skeptic Philo of Larissa; breaks with his teacher and founds a school that emphasizes the availability of knowledge—the so-called Old Academy; his amalgam of Stoic and Aristotelian ethics influences Cicero, who studies with Antiochus in Athens in 79 B.C.E.; Augustine knows of Antiochus via Cicero.

Aristotle (383–322 B.C.E.): studies at Plato's Academy some twenty years before founding his own school of philosophy, the Lyceum; a philosopher of extraordinary range and depth: logic, ethics, metaphysics, political theory, literary analysis, the sciences, and psychology. Augustine knows Aristotle's *Categories*, a work of logic, from a Latin translation; he gets bits and pieces of Aristotelian philosophy from Cicero and Plotinus. His Aristotle will always have a veneer of Stoic ethics and Platonic metaphysics.

Augustine (354–430): except for a few years in Italy, lives most of his life in Roman North Africa—Thagaste, Carthage, Hippo; bishop of Hippo from 396 until his death; writes an astounding number of works, the two most influential being *Confessions* and *City of God*; his conceptions of sin and grace profoundly inform the development of Western Christianity.

## FIGURES INVOKED

Aulus Gellius (c. 125–c. 180): Latin man of letters; grows up in Rome, where he studies literature, rhetoric, and grammar; travels to Athens to study philosophy; best known for his miscellany of anecdotes and notes on the sciences: *Attic Nights*. In *City of God* 9.4, Augustine cites and analyzes one of his anecdotes about a Stoic sage.

Caelestius (flourished early 5th century): disciple of Pelagius, shows up in Carthage soon after the sack of Rome in 410 and is refused ordination to the priesthood; he becomes a focal point for North African opposition to Pelagian theology—primarily to its denial of the heritability of Adam's guilt (original sin).

Chrysippus (c. 280–c. 206 B.C.E.): Greek philosopher from Soli; considered, along with Zeno of Citium, to be a co-founder of Stoicism; Chrysippus greatly expands and elaborates the original teachings of Zeno.

Cicero (106–43 B.C.E.): Rome's most famous orator; in the last years of his life he works to translate Hellenistic philosophy into a Latin idiom; when the young Augustine reads Cicero's *Hortensius* for the first time, he becomes, at age 18, an enthusiast for the philosophical life.

Descartes (1596–1650): French philosopher and mathematician, one of the formative minds of modern philosophy; his master work, *Meditations on First Philosophy*, treats God and soul—the traditional foci of theological speculation—as demonstrably knowable subjects. Antoine Arnauld, a logician and theologian of deep Augustinian pieties, points out to Descartes that his means of demonstrating the necessary existence of the thinking subject (the so-called *cogito*) has much in common with Augustine's response to skepticism. (The resemblance is actually superficial, as Descartes himself recognizes.)

Donatus (d. c. 355): the charismatic bishop who inspires the uncompromising form of Christianity that takes its name from him: Donatism; his succession to the See of Carthage in 313 deepens a schism within the North African church that lasts well into the fifth century. Augustine champions the Catholic side and spends a good deal of his episcopate trying to convince or compel Donatists to return to the fold.

Faustus of Milevus (flourished late 4th century): a Manichean adept with a reputation for great learning, probably only a few years older than Augustine; becomes a Manichean bishop in 382 and

## FIGURES INVOKED

leaves his wife and children. When Augustine meets him at Carthage, he likes the man personally but finds his learning hollow—the death knell for Augustine's attraction to Manicheism.

Jesus of Nazareth (*c.* 4 B.C.E.–*c.* 30 C.E.): born in Roman Palestine during the reign of Herod the Great, is baptized as a young man by John the Baptist, has a 3-year ministry in and around Galilee, dies in Jerusalem by way of crucifixion on orders from Pontius Pilate, the Roman Prefect of Judea; considered by most Christians to be the Christ, the anointed one, the only begotten son of God, the Word made flesh. As an auditor among Manichees, Augustine adopts the gnostic view of Christ and assumes that his gross material form—his physical body—is just a veil for his spirit; shortly after his disillusionment with Manicheism he takes Christ to be the epitome of a sage but not divine; by the time he writes his *Confessions*, Augustine is settled in his belief that God has become fully incarnate in Jesus Christ.

Julian of Eclanum (*c.* 380–*c.* 454): becomes bishop of Eclanum in 417, one of eighteen bishops to refuse to sign Pope Zosimus' condemnation of Pelagius and Caelestius, eventually is forced into exile; accuses Augustine of defaming marriage, confusing vice with natural desire, and generally reverting to a Manichean view of the flesh. Augustine's last, unfinished work (*c. Jul. op. imp.*) is dedicated to answering these charges.

Lucretius (*c.* 94–*c.* 50 B.C.E.): Latin poet and philosopher, best known for his epic, *On the Nature of Things*, whose hero is the atom; the poem exults scientific discipline and simple living over religious superstition, fear of death, and dreams of glory. His artfully Latinized version of Epicurean philosophy has a big influence on Virgil.

Mani (216–277): born in Persian-controlled Babylonia to a family of Aramaic speakers whose Christianity remained within Judaism; after two angelic revelations, one at age 12, the other at age 24, he takes on the task of completing the revelation he believes has been authentically but imperfectly conveyed through Buddha, Zoroaster, and Jesus; pitches his religion of light against the dark forces that imprison souls in gross matter and perpetuate ignorance. Manicheism spreads east and west after Mani falls afoul of Zoroastrian priests and the new Persian king, Bahram I, has him executed. Augustine spends about 10 years as a Manichean auditor, but as a Christian bishop he styles himself unambivalently

## FIGURES INVOKED

anti-Manichean; the Manichees known to him think of themselves as Christian.

Marcus Aurelius (121–180): the Roman philosopher-emperor, best known for his book of personal meditations on Stoic wisdom, which he writes in koine Greek while on military campaign against the German tribes.

Monnica (331–387): Augustine's mother, born into a Catholic family in Donatist Thagaste; is about 23 when Augustine is born, who is perhaps her first; Navigius, his brother, and a girl whose name is unknown are to follow. Her determination to see Augustine a Catholic Christian is legendary; even her pagan husband, the somewhat hot-tempered Patricius, bows in the end to her gentle insistences and accepts a late-in-life baptism. Shortly before her death, at the port of Ostia, she and Augustine share a mutual rapture together, a foretaste of perfect communication (*conf.* 9.10.23–25)

Paul (c. 4 B.C.E. –c. 64 C.E.): the apostle of the resurrected Christ, gets converted to the Jesus movement within Judaism soon after having a blinding vision on the road to Damascus (Acts 9:1–22); most of his ministry is to the emerging Gentile churches—the face of the new Christianity. Augustine reads Paul intensively, Romans especially, in the mid 390s, and has his view of divine–human relations fundamentally altered.

Pelagius (c. 354–c. 418): born in Britain; heads to Rome around 380, probably with the intent to study law, but ends up a worldly ascetic, filled with zeal to live and inspire the godly life of virtue; has a sojourn in North Africa shortly after Rome's fall to the Visigoths, and there he comes to the attention of Augustine and the North African bishops. His morally muscular version of Christianity gets him into trouble; he is taken to be denying human bondage to sin and therefore minimizing the need for a savior. Though cleared of heresy at the regional synod of Diospolis in 415, the North Africans never give up their animus against him. A couple of years after being condemned by two separate African councils (Milevis and Carthage in 416), he finally falls out of favor with both the Pope and the imperial court; that's the last we hear of him.

Petrarch (1304–1374): humanist of the Italian Renaissance and an avid reader of Augustine's *Confessions*; takes a pocket copy of that text—a gift from his former Augustinian confessor—to the summit of Mount Ventoux in Southern France and reads the

## FIGURES INVOKED

part where Augustine expresses wonder at his own interior depths (*conf.* 10.8.15); less given than Augustine to worldly withdraw, Petrarch will find his depths on his way to literary heights, a secular ascent.

Plato (c. 428–c. 347 B.C.E.): inventor of the philosophical dialogue, arguably of philosophy itself—as a peculiar kind of paideia. Augustine's knowledge of Plato is fragmentary and second-hand, mediated through Latin translation, excerpting, and commentary, but he gives Plato full credit for having wed the contemplative aspiration to know the real to the practical ambition of living an engaged and choice-worthy life.

Plotinus (205–270): born in Egypt, studies philosophy in Alexandria, opens his own school in Rome in 245; in addition to the singularly committed male ascetic, women and professional types are welcome; his student and friend, Porphyry, collects his writings into six sets of nine treatises—the *Enneads*—and publishes them some 30 years after his teacher's death. The vision unfolded there is, to say the least, extraordinary: a meditation on oneness, eternal mind, soul in descended and undescended forms, and the discord that is materiality. When Augustine first reads some portion of the *Enneads* in Latin translation, his sense of God fundamentally alters.

Porphyry (c. 234–c. 305): Phoenician (Lebanese) born student of Plotinus, also his editor and biographer; Plotinus saves Porphyry from a suicidal depression by noticing it, paying him an unexpected visit, and counseling him to go on holiday—he does, but as a consequence is absent when Plotinus falls sick and dies. His greatest tribute to his teacher will be his compilation and editing of the *Enneads*. He writes many things of his own as well, including a notorious critique of the Christian religion.

Socrates (c. 470–399 B.C.E.): Plato's teacher, the persona of the philosophical life; lives a life of incessant questioning, bent on knowing the good; is condemned to death in 399 B.C.E. by a majority of his fellow Athenians for worshipping gods strange to the city and corrupting impressionable minds. Augustine admires Socrates for his moral fervor, but admires Plato more for setting that fervor within a more contemplative framework.

Vincent of Cartenna: a Rogatist bishop, Rogatists being more Donatist than Catholic in their ecclesiology, but disillusioned with the violent tactics of the Donatist fringe—the so-called Circumcellions (named for their habit of congregating around small farm houses); in a lengthy letter (*ep. 93*, c. 408), Augustine recounts to Vincent his reasons for supporting imperial measures against Donatism and, by extension, Rogatism.

Virgil (70–19 B.C.E.): Rome's answer to Homer, author of the epic poem, *Aeneid*. Augustine knows Virgil well, the *Eclogues* and *Georgics* included, but it is the *Aeneid* that first informs his boyhood fancies and then shapes his theological imagination for the antithesis to God's city. Virgil's fictional ideal of an eternal empire, a *pax Romana* without end, is for Augustine a passing illusion of the *civitas terrena*, the kingdom of this world.

# PROLOGUE: A LIFE CONFESSED

*Look, my life is a stretch.*

Augustine, *Conf.* 11.29.39

Augustine was born on the 13th of November 354 in the town of Thagaste in Roman North Africa. His historical placement puts him, on the one hand, in a fallow period in the history of philosophy, at least by conventional standards, and, on the other, in one of the richest times in the history of theology. To scholars of Patristics, who study the theological formation of the early Christian church (roughly from the end of the first century to some indeterminately medieval beginning), Augustine is a titanic figure. No one in the increasingly Latinized West can rival the literary achievement of the man who wrote *Confessions, City of God*, and *The Trinity*—these being only the most celebrated items in a vast collection of writings whose depth and insight continue to this day to surprise.

Meanwhile his philosophical readers, for whom Patristics is an alien category, can barely find a way to place him at all. Augustine is too distant from Plato and Aristotle, and frankly too Christian, to be considered classical, and so he tends to be lumped in with the under-appreciated medieval figures in canonical histories of philosophy. Mostly he gets compared to Thomas Aquinas—one of the first university professors of philosophy—who, unlike Augustine, made a big point of distinguishing properly philosophical theology from extra-rational revelation. The other tendency is for Augustine to get slipped into philosophy's history as a proto-modern. Antoine Arnauld, a contemporary of Descartes and Pascal, was only the first to claim that the Cartesian discovery of an indubitable thinking self—immaterial, impersonal, and uniquely capable of knowledge—has a precedent in

Augustine's conception of a self-related mind. In general Augustine is credited with having a peculiarly modern sense of selfhood, but this usually has more to do with the agonized self-consciousness of his confessional persona than his interest in a dematerialized psyche, or with what makes him seem more like a Dostoevsky than a Descartes.

Augustine's slippery presence within the margins of philosophical canonizations makes his outsized theological stature all the more striking—but also perplexing. Is it really possible to have a highly articulate, hugely influential vision of religious possibility and not in some substantial way be cultivating a philosophy? What does it say about our intellectual culture, about us, if we find it relatively easy, even unremarkable, to tell stories about the past that partition off the history of our reverences from the history of our philosophical inquires?

I ask these questions keenly aware of the difference in cultural moment between Augustine's day and our own. He was born after the fateful conversion of emperor Constantine to Christianity but before Christianity became the only sanctioned way of being Roman. Augustine's father, Patricius (Patrick), was a pagan until soon before his death, when he accepted baptism; his mother, Monnica, grew up with a Christianity that was still mostly a cult of reverence for local saints and martyrs. As he came to his own, not always consistent, sense of a catholic faith, Augustine would have to negotiate a pluralistic mix of religious ritual and philosophical ambition, fluidly pagan and variously Christian. When he dies in August of 430, after more than 30 years as bishop of the port city of Hippo, his version of Christianity will have become, at least nominally, the imperial choice. In 380 Theodosius outdoes Constantine and makes Catholic Christianity the official religion of the Roman imperium; some 10 years later we find him outlawing pagan worship. The emperor Honorius, ruling after the partition of the empire into East and West, not only continues the imperial campaign against Rome's ancestral religions; he also weighs in against Donatism, the more home-grown form of Christianity in Roman North Africa. In 405 Honorius issues the Edict of Unity and Donatism is declared a heresy—a Christianity too defiant, too proud, too anti-Roman to be sustained. The problem for the favored form of Christianity was that its catholicity was being fitted out with the clay feet of a far-from-eternal empire. Lying on his death-bed while Vandals were blockading Hippo and preparing to besiege the city, Augustine surely knew this to be the case. We who live on the other side of Christian hegemony have the long view on the devil's pact between political power and religious affiliation; we also, as children of the genocidal twentieth century, know something about the cruelty of which secular regimes are all too capable. We live in fragilely pluralistic times, hounded by resurgent fundamentalisms and bereft of a benignly secular sanctuary. We are far from Augustine's moment.

So what can we expect from reading him again, assuming that we have grown tired of both religious nostalgia and secular indignation? I keep using the first person plural. I should come clean about my presumption. I am not writing a guide to Augustine for Christians, much less for Augustinian Christians, though I am, in more ways than not, an Augustinian Christian myself. I am not writing to convince a secular audience of the secular value of a suitably pruned Augustinianism, though I don't deny that this exercise can be of some ecumenical interest. I am writing to those who are willing to entertain the notion that the history of their reverences includes more than the history of their current allegiances. More to the point, I am writing to those who are willing to entertain this notion but are perplexed by how to do so in practice.

Philosophers generally have no trouble with the idea that it is possible to take wisdom from a Plato or a Chrysippus and not have to become a card-carrying Platonist or a Stoic. But this catholicity, admirable as it is, has a much harder time taking in more religiously identified thinkers. In the *Apology*, the dialogue that dramatizes Socrates' day in court, Plato ties his teacher's philosophical vocation to a form of religious piety; Socrates turns to philosophy out of respect for the Delphic Oracle and his faith that the god must be telling him the truth, however hard the truth may be for him to interpret. He becomes a philosopher, a true craver of wisdom, when he resolves to understand what the god *means*. I dare say that few contemporary philosophers—Platonist or otherwise—agonize much over Plato's faith in Apollo when trying to get at the meaning of Platonism. Matters are very different when it comes to Augustine. The comparatively few philosophers who include him in their catholicity make a *conscious effort* to divest his philosophy from his allegiance to his church and his love of Christ. Partly this is because of history: Christianity, not paganism, becomes the dominant, sometimes domineering, religion of Europe and its colonizing efforts. (And what is more bluntly contrary to philosophy than coercion?) Partly this is because of Augustine himself. Unlike Plato, he explicitly ties the pursuit of wisdom, or true religion, to a prior acceptance of dogmatic authority (*util. cred.* 9.21): "Apart from believing the beliefs that we later grow to understand and follow, if we acquit ourselves well and are worthy, true religion cannot, absent authority's weighty power, be rightly entered—no way." These words suggest the disposition of a religiously *identified* thinker: they exult belief over doubt, favor interpreting over knowing.

But here we need to be careful. The assumption that either consigns Augustine to a Patristics cul-de-sac or exports him unceremoniously into the Middle Ages (philosophy's Age of Faith) has him assuming beliefs without trying very hard to understand them. Imagine a hypothetical argument between two philosophers—a self-described empiricist and a faithful Augustinian. Let's grant that they have the same basic conception of how to reason. They start with premises that they deem to be true and important, and they attempt, when drawing implications, to rely as firmly as possible on the truth of the foundational premises (basically a matter of maintaining consistency). Having them begin with different premises, we can expect, given their common form of reasoning, that they will end in different places. The empiricist tells you that to be an empiricist you must begin with the premise that all knowledge is based on the senses; the farther away a claim is from verification in sense experience—e.g., the claim that God is immaterial—the less likely it is that a claim to knowledge is being made, much less a false one. The Augustinian tells you that God is the reality most worth knowing, that nothing else, like, say, the sensed world, is all that real when compared to God. To come to know God, the Augustinian continues, you must begin with the premise that the sublime father of all things, the creator of heaven and earth, has entered human awareness most intimately by way of the birth, life, death, and resurrection of Jesus of Nazareth, his only begotten son. The Incarnation is your meditative point of departure for a knowing life.

I have, for effect, made the two sides sound as alien as possible to one another, and the easiest way to do this was to make the Augustinian sound unabashedly devotional, the empiricist soberly philosophical. One way philosophers have had to adjudicate this sort of difference has been to assume that a secular premise, having no religious intonation, is readily intelligible to all (i.e., we know what makes it true or false), while a religious premise, being dressed in the language of a *particular* faith, is intelligible, if at all, only to the practitioners of that faith. But if the proper context of philosophical inquiry is cosmos and not church, philosophers being assumed to be the most cosmopolitan of thinkers, then this form of adjudication is not going to come out well for the religiously identified philosopher. Augustine will be granted philosophical credentials in as much as his vision of things can be abstracted and assessed apart from his specifically Christian commitments. As for what remains, the stubbornly sectarian part, that will define for us an Augustine who is a man of his times, socially conditioned to clip his own wings and maintain the status quo.

The minority response from within philosophy to a condescending and perhaps overly self-confident philosophical secularism has been to try to level the playing field. So what if the empiricist premise seems simpler and less culturally invested than the Augustinian alternative? Appearances can deceive. Were we to investigate the matter more thoroughly, we would discover that the foundations of the empiricist world-view are no more self-authenticating, no more self-founding, than the cardinal truths of the Christian faith. Faith-disdaining empiricists would soon begin to look less cosmopolitan and more like self-deceived sectarians. Meanwhile the self-aware Augustinians continue to acknowledge their debt to their church and philosophize with all due humility. The problem with this picture of the contest between secular and religious philosophy is that it distorts, in an all-too-tempting way, what Augustine tries to mean by church.

Suppose that you are puzzled by the choice between the empiricist and the Augustinian. Neither philosophy seems intuitively obvious to you in its foundational premise, but it strikes you that it matters, and matters a great deal, whether you live your life more like an empiricist or more like an Augustinian. You take the empiricist to be telling you that your best course in life is to ground yourself in the self-evident facts of your situation, steel yourself against the fantasies of your fears and false hopes, and work patiently to get to know the world that you have been given to know. You take the Augustinian to be telling you that your world is laced, perhaps infused, with the mystery of divinity; it has walked in your shoes, so to speak; your best course in life will be to strive humbly to discern difference between the mystery that you manufacture to keep others in their place and the mystery that comes through your compassionate desire to connect. How will you choose between these paths?

If you look to the Augustine who is writing less than 10 years past his conversion (and this includes both the leisured contemplative and the young priest), he will tell you to associate yourself with the better class of people. Let's say that the Augustinians, as a self-supporting group, prove to be more virtuous as a community than the empiricists: that will be sufficient evidence, given a view of knowledge that unifies fact and value, that the Augustinians have the better claim for the truth of their foundational premise. This early view of his, in terms of the way I have just described the options, is actually more empiricist than Augustinian: it assumes that there is a fact of the matter—the superior goodness of one person or group over another—that can be exploited to define an authentically wisdom-seeking community, a true church, and secure it against its ignorant and badly behaved rivals. He loses his hold on this kind of imperious empiricism, however, soon into his tenure as bishop of Hippo, near the beginning, that is, of his big responsibilities as a church leader. His sense of what a church is, of what it means to be either on the inside or the outside of one, changes deeply for him. He will spend the rest his life returning to that depth and attending to its mystery.

I refer to the radicalization of his doctrine of grace. Even the most pugilistic seeker of truth has to admit at the end of the day that truth is not the product of argument but is on occasion the blessing that is bestowed upon the winner of an intelligent fight; on other occasions, the winning seems to lack altogether the grace of truth—the winner's perspective being narrowed, not enhanced. There are all kinds of ways in which we are made more receptive to truth: some have us winning arguments, others losing them, some delight and uplift us with revelations of beauty, others knock us off our feet and reveal to us our blindness. The revelation that made Augustine most receptive to truth—and more or less knocked him off his feet—has been by far the most perplexing for his readers to comprehend. While working as a new bishop on a bit of Romans exegesis, Augustine reluctantly comes to the conclusion that God's favor of Jacob, the second twin out of Rebecca's womb, over Esau, his big brother—the topic of Romans 9—has nothing to do with some greater potential for virtue on Jacob's part. From the perspective of grace (what Augustine takes Paul's perspective to be), the two brothers share the same birth, despite Esau's head start in life. Esau, in other words, isn't being denied grace because of his natural gifts of strength and vitality; Jacob is being granted grace despite his apparent lack of these same gifts. The moral of the story, when shifted to the register of truth-seeking, was to Augustine both clear and unsettling: the desire for truth is not a natural virtue to be perfected and rewarded; it is a grace that compels continual transformation. Looking back on his struggle to resist this wisdom, Augustine, now an old bishop, will write (*retr.* 2.1): "I labored on behalf of the free choice of the human will, but the grace of God won out."

He does not mean to suggest that divine power obliterates human freedom—if that were so, how could he even confess to a conflict? His point is that his efforts at self-assertion, bent on earning him absolute favor and love, assume the existence of a self not yet in evidence. The ultimate source of life or the great parent that Augustine is trying to impress with his independence is still parenting him, both from within and from without, and to whatever extent Augustine has a self to assert, he has a cause for gratitude, not a demand for recognition. This qualification of his doctrine of grace does nothing, of course, to resolve the perplexity that the doctrine occasions; it makes it worse in fact. The usual complaint against the Doctor of Grace is that he undermines the rational basis of reward and punishment: his God gives us too much help when it comes to virtue and too little when it comes to vice. The real perplexity runs deeper than this. If I am to be grateful for every aspect of my being that can be considered, however meagerly, to be good, what of me is left over to express the gratitude? I would be happy and quite grateful to be able to live a life of gratitude, but wouldn't my gratitude have to be the one grace that I could not, on pain of self-contradiction, credit to God? If the grace of God preempts my freedom even to express my gratitude, I will not thereby be diminished or repressed: I simply never will have been.

Augustine becomes Augustine, a religious genius, when he shifts his manner of struggle with the great perplexity of being a self-conscious but wholly derived being. He gives less effort to the attempt to reserve for himself and the rest of us a small pocket of human initiative and more attention to an apparent paradox of ultimate power: that the God who parents humanity enters into our human genealogy as his mother's baby boy—a stunningly mundane intervention that invites each of us to receive, along with our universally divine parenting, a distinctive birth, a unique beginning. There is no contradiction between having a personality and revering oneness, not if this paradox is only apparent. But there is a fearsome struggle in human life— Augustine calls it the struggle of sin against grace—to hold onto the appearance and resolve personality into the oneness that is either jealously one or guardedly other (same difference). The church that would be a sanctuary for God's children would have to refrain from using its beliefs to divide and conquer, even as it commits itself in faith to a particular love. Augustine tries not to mean by church the institution that has the terrible responsibility for making its beliefs everyone's. He does not always succeed in this, but he never fails to remind us that the temptation to live in that impossible pocket of God-free initiative (i.e., to live in hell) is always with us in this life. Expect the church, mortal as we are, to falter.

I call him a genius not to praise him but to signal my intent to engage him where truth and force of personality are distinct but inextricable. The two ideally conjoin to reinforce and amplify one another, but their conjunction can also be a confusion that conspires with bad faith and self-deception. The essence of Augustine's perplexing faith is his confidence that the ideal is more real, more substantive than the confusion. It is impossible, he thinks, to escape the confusion, or even to want to escape it, apart from first being claimed by the ideal. That realization will always be a cause of gratitude, and in that gratitude there is both the beginning and the end of a life. Augustine's ideal of a life is of a life confessed. More often than not, confession connotes an admission of wrong-doing. When Augustine thinks of confession, he does have sin in mind, but where confession of wrong-doing subjects a person to censure or prosecution, confession of sin liberates a person from self-inflicted punishment. The more we learn to speak with God, this being the root meaning of confession, the less we will be tempted to belittle our lives and stuff them into tiny boxes of false security. The philosophical life, as Augustine conceives of it, is a lesson from life in how to petition for life. "Only those who think of God as life itself," he writes (*doc. Chr.* 1.8.8), "are able not to think absurd and unworthy things of God." And of themselves.

I lack the skill and the inspiration (and frankly the nerve) to write philosophy in the form of a prayer, but I think I understand the impetus to do so. In this guide to Augustine, the most confessional of philosophers, I will give you my best sense of this impetus and what actively resists it. Augustine is especially good at helping us see through some of the counter-forces to a life's liberation—especially the ones that masquerade as desires for self-sufficiency and moral responsibility. He is harder to follow, but still good company, when it comes to unmasking sexual desire. I will not shy away from using his best inspiration not only to clarify but also to challenge some of the things that he says. I do not do this out of any sense of having wisdom superior to his. I respect and share his view that philosophy is not about gaining the upper hand in an argument. It is about risking self for the sake of truth and a more generous self. I correct expecting to be corrected. I trust that I will expand rather than wither. I owe Augustine's spirit no less a confidence.

My guide falls into four chapters. The first two take up illusions of selfhood that he struggled to combat. One of the illusions is about self-sufficiency. Is it a reasonable wisdom to want to live outside the shadow of loss? You know that you and yours are mortal, but you work to become sufficiently secure in your self-conception to be able to accept mortality and not feel diminished. The philosophy that Augustine inherits, especially in its Romanized version, encourages him to embrace this path, but he finds himself hoping more to grieve well than not at all. The latter is an ideal, but not for this life. The other illusion of selfhood, and it has a much deeper bite for Augustine, concerns responsibility for sin. He is very tempted to embrace the notion that sin is his one absolute initiative as a human being in a God-governed world. It is a perverse initiative, to be sure—a self-defeating form of self-assertion—but it seems nevertheless an initiative that speaks to the essence of his individual responsibility. Augustine finds it much easier to share his virtue with God than share his sin. The sin-sharing seems to him disreputable for both parties. It makes him irresponsible, and it makes God out to be corrupt. Augustine will have to think very differently before he can learn to subordinate his responsibility for sin to his more fundamental responsiveness to God. When he is led into himself and into a new way of seeing, he is set to become aware of the tension between Platonism's ideal and Paul's Christ—between philosophical catharsis and the resurrection of flesh.

In the third chapter, I revisit Augustine's preoccupations with death and sin, this time within the context of his myth of origins—his reading of the story of Adam and Eve in the garden. Augustine uses this story to illustrate, but not derive, his version of the doctrine of original sin. I criticize the part of his doctrine that has sin being transmitted from parent to child by way of sexual reproduction. But I do this by way of immanent critique. It is the profundity of Augustine's own reading of Genesis that suggests why sin simply cannot be construed to be procreative. His reading tells us other things as well: about the nature of his conversion, his torment over his sexual desire, his ambivalent love of an incarnate God. This chapter is really the heart of the guide.

The last chapter, Almost an Epilogue, is a necessarily inconclusive meditation on the radicalization of grace. Augustine generally gets pegged as an eschatological thinker. This means that he expects the last things about human life—the final perfection of its form in some, its ultimate corruption in others—to happen outside the purview of historical time. In terms of what we can foresee, we can reasonably expect a lack of resolution. Yesterday's sinner is potentially today's saint, and today's saint is potentially tomorrow's sinner. The play between grace and sin, like light and shadow, infuses the time-defined world, in some sense creates it. But there is an ambiguity in Augustine's eschatology. Does he think that our human conception of the good remains perpetually open to revision over time, or does he subscribe to a largely fixed conception that awaits a final, extra-temporal fulfillment? If the latter, then Augustine would likely be identifying Christianity—or at least his version of it—with the form of the good. God would have to supply form with substance (the divine self-offering), but Augustine and his church should be able to establish the right environment for the reception of an interior grace. While I don't think that this is the best way to read Augustine, I concede that he makes this reading tempting when he gets down to the business of justifying imperial sanctions against the Donatists, whose Christianity rivaled his own. Ultimately I resist the temptation and leave him a thinker of radical grace.

I have decided, for the purposes of this guide, to engage the thought of only a few of Augustine's ancient sources. Cicero figures prominently in Chapter One, Plotinus and Paul in Chapters Two and Three, Virgil in the concluding meditation. I have made no attempt to supply a running commentary on the Augustine scholarship. Somewhat artificially, but I think justifiably, I have focused this guide on what makes Augustine perplexing and not on what makes the vast scholarship on him perplexing (a fine topic for a different book). This choice of mine should not be taken to imply that I have no gratitude for the scholarship. There are great riches there, and I have given you a treasure map of sorts in the lists of suggested readings that appear at the end of the book. I have annotated all the individual items and arranged them under headings to give you some idea, admittedly rudimentary, of the structure of Augustinian studies. Please don't assume that the books listed are just the best books, whatever best might mean, or that they are a fully representative sampling of what's out there. The field of Augustinian studies is too vast and too diverse to represent succinctly, and I have had to leave off many worthy titles. I will say that every book and essay on my collective list is well worth reading.

CHAPTER ONE

# DEATH AND THE DELINEATION OF SOUL

*It is necessary to have had a revelation of reality through joy in order to find reality through suffering. Otherwise life is only a dream—more or less bad.*

Simone Weil

The most famous line of Augustine's expansive corpus holds center stage in paragraph one of the *Confessions* (*conf.* 1.1.1): "You stir us and we delight to praise you, who made us yours—and so the heart within us is restless until it rests in you." The line is undoubtedly hopeful. The restlessness that makes an Augustine feel strange in his own skin is not native to our human condition. We humans were made, his prayer suggests, to aim at God and settle into the most delightful kind of rest. Still the hope expressed here is not without its perplexities. If the human heart is so naturally God-directed, then why the restlessness? When did we all decide to wander off on our own and paradoxically leave an eternally present God behind? Perhaps we are less keen on rest or on God than Augustine is willing to admit. And what would it mean, in any case, to rest with God, whose power to attract and upend our most settled conceptions of beauty is eternal? A life with God, though perhaps less desperate in its neediness than the alternative, seems no less needy. The Augustinian soul always needs God to live, and to live with God is to be subject to an endless call to new life.

A little later in the *Confessions* (*conf.* 1.3.5), Augustine will describe the house of his soul as a cramped space, badly in need of repair—a place too small and uninviting to be fit lodging for a being of infinite worth and perfection. In the Gospel of Matthew, a Roman centurion, worried about the health of one of his servants, petitions Jesus for help but begs him off from a house call (Matt. 8:8): "Lord, I am not worthy to have you come under my roof; but only speak the word, and my servant will be healed." Augustine, carrying the house of his ailing soul with him, is not too shy to ask for the house call. Too small a house, God? "Then let it be expanded by you." Too much of a wreck? "Rebuild it."

It is hardly news to students of theism that theists tend think of the one God as incomparably grander than his human image, however abstract or sublime the imaging. Augustine is not expecting his renovated and newly restored soul to contain the uncontainable. He writes his *Confessions* under the conviction that he lives in God if he lives at all; even when his soul appears to be roaming about in God-bereft places, he has not, strictly considered, left the many-roomed domicile of his heavenly father's house. It is God, in short, who contains him and all his life's possibilities. But it can still feel to Augustine that he has become a prodigal son, squandering his gifts in a Godless wasteland, and out of such a feeling, he can anticipate, with a mixture of joy and self-loathing, a homecoming.

The Augustinian conception of a core self, or soul, is quite unlike the idealized notion of selfhood that Augustine inherits from the philosophical schools of his day. Stoics, Epicureans, Skeptics, Platonists, and Peripatetics (followers of Aristotle) all had differing views of the highest good and differing prescriptions for how to live by it, but in the Romanized version of their philosophical diversity—mediated to him largely through Cicero, who was himself disposed to eclecticism—Augustine was able to glean a common moral: that the sign of a better wisdom is always a more secured self, a self less likely to be rent by love, wracked by grief, or confused about the source of its true power. As Augustine comes to insist on his debt to a deity who subverts his soul's prerogative of self-definition (the subversion he calls grace), he seems at the very least to be denying the possibility of a philosophically secured self. The still looming question of Augustinian studies, certainly with regard to Augustine's philosophy, is whether he denies not merely the possibility but also the wisdom of the classical ideal. If we could craft a perfect inner peace for ourselves and live untroubled by (but not necessarily indifferent to) the troubles of others, should we want that? Or is there some lesson, vital to wisdom, that comes of having a more porous self and so less of a capacity to keep others and their otherness on the outside?

Augustine will never idealize a conflicted self. He simply lacks the tragic sensibility. In the settled life he hopes to have with God—not this life but the one to come—he anticipates enjoying a happiness undarkened by the shadow of loss, and, more significantly, he anticipates an end to feeling at odds with himself. No longer will part of him want less than the happiness that his better part wants (the first Adam's problem). Of course if all that Augustine means by inner conflict is the old struggle between virtue and vice, recast as irresolvable, then his hope for an end-of-time peace will express little more than his disillusionment with philosophically prescribed self-help, the sort meant to reform less-than-virtuous desire and not simply restrain it. The philosophers most familiar to Augustine—Cicero and Plotinus especially and, from a certain point of view, Virgil—emphasize the centrality of virtue to human well-being. They do not claim that the virtuous life is easy or that virtue is all there is to happiness, but nor do they insist, as if it were some brute fact about human existence, that misbegotten desires for a bad happiness necessarily outlast anyone's personal discipline or contemplative insight. It is reasonable, say the philosophers, to hope for (if not quite expect) the perfection of virtue, the better part of happiness, in this life. But undoubtedly such hope asks for a mighty ascesis—a heroic labor of mind and will.

In one of his last writings, *The Gift of Perseverance* (*persev.* 20.53), Augustine recalls how annoyed Pelagius was at his repeated suggestion in book 10 of the *Confessions* that God has to do the work of personal discipline for us—this being our only shot at a higher life, secured against, if never entirely free from, demeaning temptations. The offending words, which, says Augustine, nearly caused Pelagius to come to blows with the bishop who was recalling them, were these (*conf.* 10.29.40, 10.31.45, 10.37.60): "Give what you command; command what you will." Pelagius was in Rome at the time; he had begun his advocacy of Christian asceticism—a secular version, since it was meant for worldly people and not just for cloistered types—in his native Britain. He left Rome for Sicily and then for Africa in advance of Alaric's attack on Rome, the sack of 410. More than Pelagius himself, his disciple Caelestius, who stayed in Carthage when Pelagius moved on to Palestine, made a bad impression on the African bishops. Caelestius questioned the African practice of infant baptism and refused to accept the doctrine that sin, like some congenital illness, mortgaged birth to moral incapacity and death.

In his view we are all much like Adam, the first human being: originally innocent, naturally mortal, able to increase our moral stock through self-exertion or diminish it through self-indulgence.

To be Pelagian in the narrow sense of the notion is to disdain Augustine's doctrine of original sin, his dread insistence on the qualitative difference between an original, but forever lost, power of moral self-determination, and the life that everyone now inherits: an antagonism of flesh and spirit, lived under a death sentence. In the broader sense, to be Pelagian is to want to preserve within Christianity, a religion of death and resurrection, some semblance of classical steadiness, the ancient confidence that we are endowed with what we need to perfect our life's promise: sufficient time (despite death) and sufficient energy (despite ills of mind and body). A typical Pelagian would underscore and not merely concede the fact that we humans live in other than ideal circumstances—Eden is definitely over. The classical sensibility, whether pagan or Pelagian, is not insensitive to adversity; it just refuses to acquiesce to it. A disciplined human being (rare as that is) can use adversity to sculpt beauty of soul.

Augustine does not always make it easy for his readers to notice the depth of his disagreement with Pelagian Christians and pagan apologists for virtue. When he reminds his pagan readers, most fulsomely in book 19 of *City of God*, that even their best philosophers still have plenty of cause to be unhappy with life, he sounds peevish. When he lets himself be goaded by Julian of Eclanum, his Pelagian gadfly, into angry indictments of carnal desire, spoiled for saints and sinners alike by Adam's fall, he sounds perverse. (It takes extraordinary loyalty to Augustine to be able to give his final diatribe against Julian, *c. Jul. imp.*—a hugely sprawling and yet unfinished work—a sympathetic reading.) Certainly the stridency of Augustine's polemics can make it seem as if he were nostalgic for life in Eden, an impression he very much needs to discredit. The Adam he takes from Genesis has an original ability not to sin (*corrept.* 12.33); such an Adam could have earned his immortality easily. All it would have taken is simple self-restraint: no eating from the forbidden tree (Gen. 2:17). Given Adam's environment of choice—plush garden, a fit partner, ready access to God—he comes off in Augustine's account as a pathetically weak-willed Pelagian. His heirs, one might hope, would be made of sterner stuff.

But Augustine does not hope for better Pelagians, and he never equates beatific peace with a restoration of Edenic conditions.

He has no nostalgia for Eden, and his Christ, the better Adam, is not better by virtue of having an infinitely enhanced ability not to sin (*posse non peccare*); on the contrary, his Christ is altogether incapable of sin (*non posse peccare*) and that is his peculiar freedom, yet to be ours (*corrept.* 12.35; cf. *ex. prop. Rm.* 13–18). Christ is, in his humanity, the perfection that comes of having God fully enter one's house and remake it from within. The result is not an architectural miracle of stability but an enduring mystery of rebirth without repetition.

Much more so than their modern successors, the philosophers of antiquity tend to identify fear of death as the singular challenge to the life well lived. One can understand why. If I see myself as being in the business of perfecting my own life, I am likely to be more confident about initiating this business than securing the time I need to bring it to completion. My virtue, such as it is, may be my own, but I have many reasons—all bearing on the vulnerability of my mortal frame—for thinking that my time is not. If I start to worry more about my time and less about my virtue, I risk becoming enamored with false images of my life's perfection.

To take an example dear to the heart of ancient moralists, I may come to mortgage my power of self-determination to a craving for fame. Suppose that I do something fantastically memorable: I defeat an enemy in battle who was by all odds destined to defeat me. If others assume that I did so by virtue of my ingenuity or courage and not just by dumb luck, then I will win their admiration and my whole life may come to be associated in their minds with that defining moment of glory. The problem with this image is less my expectation that I will live on long after my death in the memory of others than my willingness to define the worth of my virtue in terms of someone else's regard. Although it is a proper part of virtue to be able to recognize and appreciate virtue in others (Aristotle thought of this as the basis of true friendship), it is not a power of virtue to be able to *produce* that effect. I cannot cause you to value me for my virtues; I can only hope that you will have sufficiently cultivated your own virtues so as to be in a position to enjoy and celebrate mine. And while I can rightly take some pleasure from your virtuous esteem of me, I cannot afford, on pain of self-contradiction, to make that esteem part of my self-definition. I am essentially what I have made myself to be at this moment, however you may see me. As for the time ahead of me, I will try to live in the knowledge that death—not only my own, but yours as well—has no bearing on my essential well-being.

The most shocking aspect of Pelagianism to the likes of an Augustine is its acceptance of the naturalness of death. The Pelagian Adam, formed by God out of moist clay, is as mortal as any earthen creature; he cannot hope to escape death by way of steadfast or superior virtue. His descendents differ from him only in the manner of their mortal beginning, all being born of women. Augustine tells a different story. He sees death as an evil and a punishment, one that may be put to good use by a good God, but never with the result of making an evil essentially good (*civ. Dei* 13.4). Given the close association in mortal life between birth and death (the one leading ineluctably to the other), Augustine will find it hard to make death an evil without also tainting the goodness of birth. But death for him is not finally an *unqualified* evil, and despite what his Pelagian critics may have thought about his doctrine of original sin, he was not reverting to his one-time adherence (though never wholehearted) to a Manichean form of Christianity, where flesh is made out to be the antithesis of spirit and not its alienated partner. Be that as it may, the Pelagians who irked Augustine were hardly modern-day naturalists attending to the rhythms of loss and gain in a life; they were Christian participants in an antique strategy, astoundingly versatile, of indifference to death.

Philosophers as different as Lucretius, a philosopher-poet and Epicurean of the late Roman Republic, and Marcus Aurelius, a philosopher-king and Stoic of the Roman Empire, could find common cause on this issue. Out of vastly different assumptions about the order of things (chance versus providence), they and their philosophical kin were moved to dissociate death from loss: to their person of wisdom, the only loss that counts is the self-willed loss that results in ignorance and vice. Think of it this way: death and disease may reduce you to a disorganized heap of insentient elements, but as long as your sentience remains naturally supported, you can create for yourself a virtuous identity, superimposed upon the natural, that then becomes your truth. Your eventual death may either remove your truth from the visible order or erase you altogether (here the philosophers disagree), but no natural diminisher has the power to separate you from your virtue. Brute nature lacks such discrimination. When Pelagian Christians affirm the naturalness of death and seem to have no use, much less feeling, for the God who dies, they join the antique consensus about virtue that Augustine has come to reject.

Most of us labor under the impression that we have more to lose in life than our virtues. Time has an unnerving way of removing the cultivation from our lives and returning us to simpler needs–perhaps a parting reminder of death's complicity with birth. But the pressing question for us, by ancient lights, is not whether we are subject to more than self-willed loss, but whether we ought to make a virtue of that recognition. Perhaps, after all, it is only the trying, the attempt at cultivation, that matters. The man who prays, "Give what you command," obviously thinks not, but what manner of thinking is this, if it is not to be, by the old Roman standards, merely a resigned and unmanly capitulation to naked human need?

Augustine's offering to philosophy of a wiser, if less self-controlled, sense of loss is the biggest clue to his own, strikingly unclassical, delineation of soul. I use the word clue and not a word like revelation because it is far from obvious what the nature of the grief is that is better suffered than transcended. No doubt it is remarkable, given the influence on him of the ancient schools, that Augustine thinks it appropriate for a wise person to grieve at all. Still we have to sort out the difference within his new paradigm between an affected grief and genuine loss-taking. That task defines much of the work of the remainder of this chapter. I begin with a closer look, via Cicero, at the philosopher's critique of grief and then take up Augustine's basic critique of that critique; from there I examine Augustine's confessional reformulation of an unsettling passion. The broader issue, extending into other chapters, concerns the value of the life that makes a person liable to grief.

## VIRTUE COMES TO GRIEF

### Ciceronian plot

In mid-February of 45 B.C.E., Cicero's only daughter, Tullia, to whom he was deeply attached, died at his country estate at Tusculum, near Rome, owing to complications of childbirth; her child died about a month thereafter. Cicero stayed away from Tusculum for several months and effectively dropped out of public life, despite the gentle urging of his longtime friend, Atticus, who wanted him to put on a brave face and continue to meet his obligations as a leading citizen. Aside from this being the general expectation of a *vir optimus*, a great man, his friend's advice was politically prudent: Julius Caesar held power in Rome, and Cicero's one-time support of Pompey,

Caesar's defeated rival, was, though forgiven, certainly not forgotten. In his letters from that time of withdrawal, Cicero reassures Atticus that he has not been wasting away but writing with great intent, turning sorrow into contemplation. Most of Cicero's major philosophical writings were indeed to follow in the wake of Tullia's death, among them a work of consolation, now lost. Cicero tells Atticus that he was able, through self-consolation, to diminish the outward show of his grieving (*ep. 267*, 12.28): "The grief itself," he adds, "I was not able to lessen, nor would I want to, were I able."

Augustine knew of Cicero's *Consolatio*. He invokes the work in *City of God* (*civ. Dei* 19.4) as the paradigm expression of the genre. But his intent is not to praise Cicero as a writer; it is to underscore the incapacity of even the best wrought words to take in, much less away, the sum of human suffering. The Cicero of the letters, writing to a close friend, might have been disposed to concede the point, even adding that no one should have supposed otherwise. But in a work styled as a series of philosophical conversations, written while still in mournful seclusion at Tusculum and intended for a wider audience, Cicero defends a more traditional conclusion. In book 3 of *Tusculan Disputations*, the main speaker works to convince one of his companions that wisdom is the cure for all manner of mental distress (*aegritudo*), grief included. The wise person is, in the classic meaning of the word, apathetic—not insensible or dead inside but free of the kind of passion (Greek, πάθη; Latin, *perturbatio*) that wrecks a person's reasoned self-possession and gives reign to bad judgment.

To feel the force of Cicero's argument it is important to know something about his theory of emotions. He lays out that theory, broadly Stoic, in book 4 of *Tusculans*. Emotions have four basic forms and two basic objects, he explains: desire (*libido*) and abandon (*laetitia*) have as their object pleasure and its pursuit; fear (*metus*) and distress (*aegritudo*) relate to pain and its avoidance. When I seek a pleasure that moves me to abandon my good sense, I am in a state of desire; when I shrink from a pain I assume will be self-rending, I am in a state of fear. The Latin terms in the parentheses are all terms of art for Cicero; they are meant specifically to designate emotions in their primitive, untutored state, the assumption being that emotions admit of refinement and even transformation. The well-tempered psyche experiences resolve (*voluntas*) but not desire, gladness (*gaudium*) but not abandon, reserve (*cautio*) but not fear.

"It seems to me," writes Cicero (*Tusc.* 4.31.65), "that all the theorizing about emotion comes down to this: that emotions are all in our power, that all of them express judgment, that all are voluntary." His principal term for emotion, *perturbatio animi*—literally a mental disturbance, already connotes the malady of those who neglect their education and fall into bad habits of judgment (for which they have only themselves to blame). Cicero will need a new word to designate well-heeled feelings of resolve, gladness, and reserve. He calls them constancies (*constantiae*; *Tusc.* 4.6.11 f.); more than rational emotions, they are the very embodiments of reason.

As the one form of emotion that is essentially uneducable, distress rates its own discussion. The word that Cicero uses for distress, *aegritudo*, is usually not restricted to mental vexation but can also mean, as Augustine points out while pondering this part of Cicero (*civ. Dei* 14.7), bodily illness and physical torment. But Cicero is not claiming that it is irrational for a person of wisdom to get sick or feel pain. He is claiming that none of the assaults on mortal flesh need ever become a *reason* for feeling distressed. There is no good reason for mental distress of any kind, and as a master of reasons, a wise person will not think or feel differently. Here is the key passage from book 3 of *Tusculans* (*Tusc.* 3.34.82–83):

> All distress is far removed from the wise person, being that it is empty, that it is a pointless experience, that it has its source not in nature but in judgment, in opinion, in a certain call to grief that comes whenever we resolve that grieving is called for. With the wholly voluntary element removed, distress will be taken away, the grievous part—but still the mind will feel a bite and be contracted a bit.

Note the curious reference to an involuntary contraction of mind, sometimes confused with distress proper, but on analysis very different. Cicero was well aware of the debate between the Peripatetic and Stoic schools of philosophy over whether a person of wisdom would ever be *completely* beyond the reach of distressful emotions. The Peripatetics thought not. They put some value on objects of desire that, once lost, were nothing other than involuntary losses. Moral virtue was not in this boat, but physical beauty and fitness, loved ones, and material wealth were. In short, much of what many of us would consider crucial to happiness counted for the Peripatetics as external goods (*bona externa*), the loss of which would be in some way distressing. The Stoics preferred to call such things preferable items (*praeposita*); they could, like moral goods, elicit commitment, but the true sage—presumptively Stoic—would be able to dissent from the commitment if the preferable were lost and, in retrospect, undo a preference. Just imagine a Stoic Cicero, confronting the loss of Tullia. Like most fathers, he naturally prefers not to survive his daughter, but having survived her, he engages in self-therapy and comes to the conclusion that her loss to him is not a loss to his virtue; he is still, as he was when she lived, essentially himself. The involuntarily pain of loss that precedes his conclusion and then survives it as an occasional physical echo is not, from the Stoic point of view, an emotion; it is more like a toothache or a cut—something that hurts (and so causes the mind to contract) but conveys no grief.

It is not clear from the quoted passage whether Cicero is siding with one of the two schools over the other. Though usually keen to find Latin equivalents for Greek philosophical terms, he does not give a name to the involuntary contraction of the mind that a Greek Stoic writing after Chrysippus, the great Stoic systematizer, would have termed a pre-passion (προπάθεια). So perhaps Cicero was not intending that kind of conceptualization. In his compendium of classical ethics, *The Ends of Things Good and Bad*, finished shortly before he began *Tusculans*, he seems ready to follow the lead of his old teacher, Antiochus of Ascalon, who considered the differences between Peripatetics and Stoics on the matter of losable goods (and attachment thereto) more verbal than real. "What difference does it make," Cicero asks, obviously impatient with Stoic novelty (*fin.* 4.9.23), "whether you call wealth, power, health goods (*bona*) or preferred items (*praeposita*), when the one who calls them goods gives them no more value than you who dub them preferred?" But despite the rhetorical nod to a Peripatetic ecumenism in ethics, where virtue suffices for happiness while virtue with added value suffices better, Cicero goes on to criticize Antiochus for inconsistency (*fin.* 5.27.81–82): how can a best life be made better? If virtue suffices, then it suffices.

To speak of virtue as sufficient for happiness is to think of virtue as the perfection of selfhood and not as one kind of good, albeit a superior kind, among others. It is not possible to add to perfection and get something better. Hence Cicero in *Tusculans* 3, still on the topic of grief, feels free to advance the cause of self-love as it were a truth of reason (*Tusc.* 3.29.73):

> It is a lustrous thing and, if you look into it, a thing also right and true that we should love as much as we love ourselves those who claim our affections most. More than that is not doable. In friendship it is not even desirable that my friend love me more than himself or I him more than me. If such were the case, it would be the disordering of life and all of its proper offices.

Think of those who face the prospect of their own deaths calmly but become unhinged when facing the death of someone they love. What some may see as a laudable loss of self-regard Cicero characterizes above as a pathological inconsistency. If my virtue depends upon me, then my death—which is mostly out of my control—is no threat to my self's perfection. Similarly the death of a loved one is no threat. If I were to treat it as a threat, I would not be expressing a love greater than my self-regard; I would be corrupting myself.

As far as I can tell, the quasi-Stoic philosophy that Cicero comes to profess does not require him to deny his grief. He is not being inconsistent when he confides to Atticus that he wants to live with the loss of his daughter and not be done with it. He clearly considers his pain a memorial to something of value. But what good has been lost? His philosophy will not let him say that Tullia was his virtue. The false belief whose ouster would have left him pained but still in possession of himself is presumably this: that one person can be materially implicated in the virtues of another—as if a root power of self-determination were made subject through mutual affection to the meeting and parting of bodies. Cicero, with his virtues intact, takes in an undefined loss. His willingness to call that loss the loss of a good leaves his philosophy of grief caught between an impulse to trivialize (the loss, not being a loss of virtue, is nothing at all) and a disposition to despair (the loss, not being a loss of virtue, is beyond measure). It takes an Augustine to want to focus philosophy there, on the agony of virtue itself.

## Augustinian dénouement

Augustine credits his philosophical awakening to Cicero. He tells us in the *Confessions* (*conf.* 3.4.7) that he was only 18 when he read

Cicero's *Hortensius* and that the book changed his affect (*affectum*). He started to look for wisdom from life and not for the vanities that tend to please most other passionate, intellectually gifted, sexually driven, politically ambitious young men who are experiencing big-city life for the first time. His new affect had its work cut out for it. Augustine had left his native Thagaste, an inland town in the farm-belt of Roman North Africa for Carthage, the Punic Rome. Looking back he describes his adolescent entry into bigger theater in memorable terms (*conf.* 3.1.1): "I came to Carthage, and a frying pan of unsavory loves sizzled around me on all sides. I didn't have love yet; I was in love with love, and from a more hidden place of need I hated the less needy me." Not exactly a sentiment that rushes a person toward Stoic resolve, Peripatetic virtue, or some judiciously Ciceronian amalgam of the two. Augustine's personal choice of a philosophy at the time—one that would see him through his twenties—was that of Manicheism, the religious inspiration of the third-century Mesopotamian prophet Mani, who lived and died under Persian rule.

Manicheism is best known for its dualistic cosmology of conflicting forces, light and dark—two kingdoms with a contested border. The dark side, vice-driven and grossly material, succumbs to envy and decides to invade the light, consequently trapping light in matter and giving birth to the debased material order of our current human experience. The kingdom of the light responds in various ways, most notably by sending along a Jesus who, unlike his material impersonator, can remind beings forgetful of their luminescence whence they come. Awakened to this knowledge, the Manichean Elect work with less self-knowing but still promising assistants—the Hearers—to disencumber light from matter. The work can take on a peculiarly material cast, as sainted luminaries obsess over their diets. No meat-eating for saints, but also no eating of any vegetables they have picked for themselves. Augustine, a former Hearer of the sect, recalls having persuaded himself of some manifestly bizarre beliefs (*conf.* 3.10.18): "that a fig weeps when picked and that its mother, the fig-tree, weeps tears of milk; that if some saint were to eat the fig, the picking being someone else's sin, not his, he would digest it and breathe out angels, or better yet, retch up God-bits in a belched prayer."

Never popular with Roman stalwarts, who viewed its association with Persia (the "decadent" East) with suspicion and contempt, Manicheism was in the eyes of many Catholic Christians an arch-heresy.

It was, from the beginnings of its missionary reach into Roman territories in the late third century, a secretive movement, existing in tight groups on the margins of society. As a newly installed bishop, writing in part to reassure his readers of his ex-Manichean standing, Augustine had reason enough to paint his former years of allegiance as a time of temporary insanity, when he had come to believe in the grotesque. He encourages his readers to forget that the distance between Cicero and Mani was once remarkably short in his mind and that his turn to the religion of Mani was motivated by his desire, however immature, to be less worldly and live more philosophically. His brief description in the *Confessions* of his newly changed affect is telling, but it stops short, I think, of being explicitly self-revealing.

What he tells us is that Cicero opened him to a new love, to the wisdom that is the property of no school or sect, but is, as divine, indivisible and eternally beautiful. He assumed that Christ—the name his mother had taught him from his earliest days to revere—was the divine name for this wisdom, and so he naturally turned his attention to the Gospels and the rest of scripture, looking there for something resonantly Ciceronian. And here is where his affection for Cicero's style of writing got him into trouble. He was put off by the apparent crudeness of the Bible—especially the older portions, where a jealous divinity, having body parts, seemed to countenance such things as polygamy and tribal warfare. "It was my self-inflation," he concedes, looking back (*conf.* 3.5.9), "that was refusing the Bible's manner, and my insight never reached down to its inner depths." While still surface-minded, he eagerly wanted to believe the Manichees when they assured him that Mani's revelation, tied to the divinity in Christ but divorced from childish anthropomorphisms and worldly values, rested on no other authority than truth itself (*conf.* 3.6.10): "They used to say, 'truth!, truth!,' and they said many things to me about the truth, but the truth was never in them."

It would be more than a decade before Augustine would meet and spend extended time with Faustus of Milevis, a Manichee with a reputation for big learning. When that meeting finally took place, it marked the beginning of the end of Augustine's Manichean sojourn (*conf.* 5.6.11 f.). He ended up liking Faustus and even admired him for how open and unassuming he could be about the limits of his learning. But those limits surprised Augustine. Faustus had a conventional but hardly deep knowledge of the liberal arts—some Cicero and Seneca, a smattering of poetry, good rhetorical skills.

"It is indeed possible for someone ignorant of the arts to have a grip on spiritual truth, but not," Augustine wryly notes (*conf.* 5.7.12), "if that person is a Manichee." When Augustine took his leave of both Faustus and Carthage and headed, at age 30, for Rome and new philosophical frontiers, the impression we are left with as readers of the *Confessions* is that he was leaving most of his Manichean craziness behind him. The assumption that had once given him leave to move from Cicero to Mani had become weak and untrustworthy. No longer could he confidently assume that soul-satisfying wisdom is the fruit of intellectual sophistication, enthusiastically culled from any available source. He arrives in Rome still a well-reputed professor of rhetoric, but bone-tired of his all-too-worldly success. For a while he falls in with Academic skeptics, philosophers who could boast Cicero as their distinguished forebear, but who, in Augustine's understanding of them at the time, had wisely given up on wisdom: "I began to think then," he writes (*conf.* 5.10.19), "that the philosophers known as Academics were shrewder than the rest—because they took account of the doubtfulness of everything and determined that nothing about the truth is humanly graspable."

Augustine's path from Cicero to Mani and through Manicheism finally dead-ends for him in a debilitated skepticism: the eclectic openness to wisdom, urged in the *Hortensius,* has become virtually indistinguishable in his mind from a disposition not to commit wholeheartedly to anything. Along the way Augustine has had his Carthage years of luxuriant exoticism, when he seemed willing to believe just about anything provided that the belief was coiffed in the rhetoric of truth-seeking. The moral to take from all this may well be that the desire for wisdom, when made to serve some combination of curiosity and a need to appear persuasive, is apt to make the most talented of persuaders, like the rhetorical Augustine, irresponsible and even a touch stupid. For what, after all, is the Manichean postulate of a dark and foreign soul, crudely encasing the light that one is, but a fanciful invitation to skip the moral cultivation part of becoming enlightened? A soul of light is, by its very nature, *already* enlightened; all the dark stuff that binds its awareness is just an alien impediment to its self-knowledge—a problem that a better diet and a less materially invested lifestyle are presumably able to solve. In his writings directed specifically against the Manichees, Augustine will be tireless in his insistence that they have confused bad habits with an evil nature. Or as he explains in *Two Souls: An Anti-Manichean Work* (*duab. an.* 13.19):

"So it happens that when we strive for better things and run up against the habits of flesh and sin that begin in some way to make trouble for us, some fools suspect, out of the dumbest of superstitions, that there is a kind of soul not of God." There is no naturally bad soul, Augustine has come to see; there is only the good soul that has hobbled itself through a history of bad judgment.

But despite Augustine's inclination in his anti-Manichean writings to make moralism into the alternative to Manichean dualism—an inclination that much delighted his eventual Pelagian critics—it is arguable that he was never moving from an exotic form of moral indigence to an unsentimental, chiefly Roman, form of self-sculpting (and then back again, if his Pelagian critics are to be believed). In his mind there was just not a profound difference and certainly no incompatibility between his rejection of Manichean psychology (where sin gets misconceived) and his reaction against Pelagian moralism (where grace is missed). They were simply the two different sides of his single-minded philosophy of sin and grace. "For it is one thing," he writes (*retr.* 1.9.2.), "to wonder where evil gets its start, another thing to wonder where the return to innocence begins, or the attainment of something greater."

Admittedly the compatibility, much less the complicity, of his two critiques—one of Manichean vice, the other of Pelagian virtue—has been far from obvious to his readers, the sympathetic ones included, who have used the *Reconsiderations*, his late-in-life review of his major works, as their guide. In his review of *Two Souls*, for example, he reconsiders the definition of sin that the Pelagian bishop, Julian of Eclanum, once described as a piece of gold in a dung-heap (*retr.* 1.15.4; cf. *c. Jul. imp.* 1:44): "Sin is the will to retain or acquire what justice forbids—an injustice from which one is free to abstain." Augustine holds to the basic truth of his definition but restricts freedom to abstain from injustice to Adam, who sins anyway. Adam's mortal heirs—all of humanity save Jesus and perhaps Mary—are born predisposed to injustice and can be expected to live out this predisposition in fact, barring infant death or divine intervention. Little wonder that Augustine's sense of sin's penalty (*poena peccati*) could evoke a Manichean-like fear of the flesh.

I am nevertheless still inclined to believe that the deeper truth lies with the complicity of his critiques. In the manner of his break from the Manichees, Augustine does indeed bar his own door to a Pelagian alternative. To see this, we need to consider more thoroughly what

Augustine comes close to revealing in the *Confessions*: that his turn to the religion of Mani was his answer to Cicero's call to the philosophical life.

The *Hortensius* was a work of Cicero's last years, written after the death of his daughter and as part of his self-prescribed literary therapy. Although only fragments of the exhortation have survived (in the form of quoted material), it is reasonable to assume that Cicero underscored there, as elsewhere, the cardinal offering of philosophy: that the person of a truly philosophical disposition can learn to weather adversity and apparent defeat and remain wholly intent on serving the highest good. Being himself a lover of republican values and a great believer in the promise of politics, Cicero doubtless would have found little to love in the apolitical asceticism of the Manichees, whose kingdom of light was not of this world. Still Cicero was not unfamiliar with extreme forms of the desire to dematerialize value— nor was he entirely unsympathetic to the impulse.

I mean by the dematerialization of value the perfect dissociation of a good from its material bearer. If the material bearer is lost, the good remains or may even be said to be liberated. Cicero's Stoics practice one kind of dematerialization when they refuse to call goods that can be involuntarily lost good (*bonum*); they are preferred until they are lost—then they are viewed, in retrospect, to have been of indifferent value. (And so the Stoic: "I lost my friend to death, but not the virtue I brought to that friendship; it is the virtue that I must continue to value and not the perishable thing whose presence I once preferred and can no longer have.") The Manichees, whom Cicero never knew as such, practice another kind of dematerialization: because they consider materiality a foreign *constraint* on goodness, they have to insist even more emphatically than do the Stoics that no material loss is ever really a loss. It is, on the contrary, victory over an enemy. (And now the Manichee: "I haven't lost my friend to death; the realm of darkness has lost one of its kidnapped lights. Years before his so-called death, my friend recognized his true nature in this life—really this death of a life—and lightened his tread: no children for him, no amassment of wealth and property, no violent consumption of flesh. He left behind tracks that only children of the light can follow.") Cicero clearly disliked overzealous and convoluted attempts to deny loss in life, but he had his own proclivity to dematerialize virtue—even as he held tight to a private grief.

My point is this. When Augustine disavows his Manicheism, he stops looking to isolate his self-formation from all the possible sources of grief in his life. The Manichean mode of this strategy—extreme and probably impossible to pull off in practice—is to darken matter and live as if the external world were constituted by a loss of light and lightness, a loss of self. This leaves the remainder self, the soul of light, surrounded on all sides by a grief it has resolved not to feel. The other extreme of a dissociative ethic—that of Stoic placidity (ἀπάθεια)—looks for reasonableness from the natural order and thus stands a pole apart from Manichean world-weariness. Every Stoic sage feels at home in the world, while every Manichean saint feels at home somewhere else. Before he knew much about grief-denying philosophy and its antipodal forms, Augustine was looking for the name of Christ in a philosophy: he found it first in Manicheism. It was a long association for him, but as strange as he made it sound, the real question is why the ex-Manichee failed to find in Pelagian Christianity the sage-like Christ of his hopes. Pelagians saw themselves as the reasonable alternative to Manichean extremism.

Here I will make use of the analogy between Stoic and Manichean asceticism as a wedge into Augustine's way of thinking. Obviously those two forms of the ascetic life speak to very different notions of the human condition, and from the standpoint of our own day, Manicheism is too wildly speculative and under-argued to rate as a philosophy, whereas Stoicism has classical credentials and an undisputed place of importance in the subsequent evolution of the philosophical canon. But the prejudice against the very notion of a Manichean philosophy will not help us a whit to understand Augustine, who would have seen in the happiness-bestowing virtues of the Stoics and the gnostic fantasies of the Manichees two forms of the same philosophically seductive idea: that wisdom is the privilege of secured selfhood. A self is insecure if it has reason to fear the involuntarily loss of whatever good gives it its ideal self-definition. If I am a Manichean saint, then I get beyond fear of self-loss when I remember that I am already, in my essence, the good that I seek (though there is still that delicate matter of rejoining my light to the greater light); if I am a Stoic sage, then I am beyond such fear once I identify my good with the perfect good of the whole cosmos, of which I am an integral part (though there is still that delicate matter of my particular preferences). When Cicero criticizes Stoics for being disingenuous about their preferences, he is suggesting a fairly modest revision of their idealized cosmos: the world, such as it is, supports virtue, but virtue is not all there is to happiness. A truly ideal order would fully support both virtue and the preferences of virtuous people—basically a Pelagian heaven. If we are looking for some sign of a Pelagian mind-set in the anti-Manichean Augustine, we may reasonably expect to find it in his post-Manichean affinity for Cicero and Cicero's critique of Stoicism (Pelagius being to Mani roughly what Cicero is to a Stoic). By the same token, lack of affinity would tell us something about the depths of Augustine's animus against anything resembling the classical ideal of virtue.

In book 9 of *City of God,* in a section devoted to the passions of a person of wisdom (*civ. Dei* 9.4), he sounds very Ciceronian at first. He divides philosophical opinion on the passions into two schools—Stoic and Peripatetic—and then endorses Cicero's judgment about the difference between them: that it does not matter whether involuntarily lost goods are called goods or something else. Involuntary loss will be involuntarily felt, regardless of a person's level or form of wisdom. But Cicero's motive for assimilating the Stoic to the Peripatetic point of view was to underscore the overriding importance of virtue to a philosopher's self-definition. Attachment to other kinds of goods has some register in the emotions, but never, says Cicero, as the kind of distress that ruins the integrity of virtue and sows division into a sage's self-understanding. Augustine, for his part, is ready to acquiesce to a tattered virtue.

For his illustration of the Ciceronian point of view, he chooses an anecdote from *Attic Nights*, the miscellany of Aulus Gellius, an enthusiast of Greek philosophy who lived in the second century. Gellius describes having been on board ship with a famous Stoic who turned pale with fright when a powerful storm started to rage. After the seas had calmed, Gellius asked the sage why he blanched at the prospect of losing what was not his choice to retain. The Stoic explained that everyone is subject to involuntary impressions (Φαντασίαι) of imminent loss or gain—these come too quickly to be helped; the person of wisdom, however, knows to consent only to what is truly of value in any given situation: the opportunities for virtue. If the idea here is that the Stoic was able to externalize his fear and call it, in retrospect, a meaningless bodily agitation, then Augustine is clearly not buying (*civ. Dei* 9.4): "Surely if the philosopher in the story were giving no weight to what he felt he was about to lose by shipwreck—his life and limb—he would not have shrunk so from the danger as to pale in fear." Augustine accepts the Stoic idea that emotions, being deposits of resolve (*voluntates; civ. Dei* 14.6), always convey judgments of value, but he denies that Stoics or anyone else can lay claim to a consistent mode of appraisal. No form of revisionism, however benign, can unify judgment. And so where Cicero reaffirms virtue's integrity in the face of involuntary bodily agitations (call them what you will), Augustine finds a perpetually divided house. Philosophers, just like the rest of us fools, experience value in contradictory ways.

Augustine does seem to entertain the idea that the ideal of Stoic placidity and unity of resolve may be realized, if not here, then in the life to come (*civ. Dei* 14.9). Certainly there will be no cause for grief, he thinks, when the soul is fully basking in the love of God, and even if love may not cast out fear in *all* of its forms (cf. 1 Jn. 4:18), the beatified fear that remains is no servile or mundane thing. But Augustine is offering no more than a tentative speculation about the transformation of all the basic emotions, save grief, into beatified forms, and in any case his eschatological frame of mind tends to obscure the extent of his divergence from all the various forms of moralism that were known to him: Ciceronian, Pelagian, Stoic, and Manichean. The real issue for him is not whether a saint struggling in the earthly vale is Stoicism's sage in the afterlife. It is whether a person of perfect wisdom, while still in his life, ever has reason to grieve. On that issue, Augustine takes his stand with the Gospels. Jesus wept for his friend Lazarus (Jn. 11:38), and in his garden agony at Gethsemane, he nearly grieved himself to death (Matt. 26:38). Augustine has no doubt about how such ascriptions of feeling to Jesus—wisdom incarnate—are to be read. They are literally true (*civ. Dei* 14.9): "The human emotion was not fake in him who had a genuine human body and a genuine human mind."

There is nevertheless a difference between Christ's experience of humanity and the humanity that the rest of us experience—and it is a difference that counts when it comes to grief. Augustine notes that when we give into grief, we often do so involuntarily, even when we know that we would be grieving out of love (*caritas*) and not some blameworthy motive (*cupiditas*). He surmises from this that grief and other involuntary passions have their origin in the infirmity of our human condition: "but it is not like this," he adds (*civ. Dei* 14.9), "for the Lord Jesus, whose infirmity originated from his power."

Although the contrast is doubtless important, it is not clear at first what Augustine intends by it. Does he mean that Christ's grief expresses his divine self-control and not his human vulnerability? Unlikely. Grief that is wholly willed is affected and therefore fake. Christ's grief, Augustine assures us, is not fake. What about the rest of us? If we resist surrendering to even a charitable grief, is the implication that we prefer to will rather than to feel? The moralist in me is inclined to answer, "yes, but so what?" It is Augustine himself who suggests to me that I ought to be grieving mostly for sin—mainly my own, but also that of others, whom I am learning to love as myself. Grieving for sin is what Christ, as both the sinless human being and the God of love, does more authentically than anyone else. So perhaps the difference between his grief and ours may be put this way: he defines the meaning of our grief; we do not define the meaning of his. Not being Christ, I can always count on having more moral work to do before I feel the right grief. And yet my inner moralist, still annoyed, persists: "Why isn't exhortation rather than grief the better response to sin in others, repentance rather than grief the better response to sin in myself?"

The answer to this, if there is one, is that grief over sin is less a response to moral failure than a recognition of loss. If I take my lessons from Augustine, who is careful to single out grief (*tristitia*) from other kinds of distress (*dolor, aegritudo*), I will learn that I lose others more profoundly to sin than I do to death. I will also learn that I have no claim to this awareness and, in a sense, no right to it, while lost to sin of my own. Most profoundly I will learn that a human teacher, even as good a one as Augustine, is not the real teacher here; for either the lesson of grief and its remedy is confessional—intimately a matter of give-and-take between God and soul—or ethics is, from an Augustinian point of view, an absent-hearted and empty moralism. I turn now to confessional matters.

## THE MATERIALIZATION OF LOSS

### Trappings of woe

Augustine is remarkably preoccupied in the *Confessions*, the early books especially, with the authenticity of his feelings. In book 1 he recalls his boyhood love of Virgil's *Aeneid* and faults himself for having wept back then for Dido, the anti-hero who kills herself when heroic Aeneas, her lover and (in her mind) husband, favors his divine calling to found a new Troy in Rome over a less fated life with her in Carthage: "What then is more pitiable," he asks (*conf.* 1.13.21), "than a pitiful man with no self-pity? He weeps for Dido, dead from loving Aeneas, but not for himself, dead from not loving you, God, light of my heart, bread of my soul's mouth, power that weds my mind to my thought's inmost chamber (*sinus*)." The implication of Augustine's self-indictment—cast curiously as a kind of autopsy—is that he was grieving for the wrong person, albeit a fictional person. In book 3, where he looks back at his Carthage years, he is more generally concerned by how theatrical he was becoming on the inside, in the sinuses of his soul (*conf.* 3.2.2): "I was captivated by stage plays, full of images of my own miseries, fuel to my fire." He wonders why anyone, himself included, would choose to be entertained by staged suffering and death. There must be some pleasure at stake, he surmises, but a pleasure that is peculiarly indebted to pain: "If human calamities, whether historical (*antiquae*) or unreal (*falsae*), are acted out in such a way that the spectator is not pained, he storms out of the theatre disgusted and disapproving; but if pained, he stays transfixed and enjoys his weeping."

If an affect is false to its core, then its transfer from one object to another—say from Dido to God—is not going to improve matters. Remember that Augustine holds to the theory that emotions reflect judgments, though often not very deliberate ones, about what is worth having or avoiding. On this score he seems more consistent than the Stoics, who hold to the same theory but allow their sages the out of dispensable pre-passions or impressions. A pleasure or pain, experienced (let us stipulate) as a pure sensation, unfiltered through belief, would not count for Augustine as an emotion or even an impression of an emotion. The Stoic who accidentally stubs his toe is not (necessarily) having an emotion, but the one who involuntarily fears for his life because of some perceived danger most certainly is. Where the mind is stirred, emotion too must be present—emotion being by definition a stirring up or disturbing of the mind (*perturbatio animi*). In keeping with this definition, it is one order of distress to have your body cut, battered, and burned; quite another to have your mind keyed to insecurity, loss, and despair. Experience of the first order of distress can of course give rise, in a thinking being, to experience of the second (pains being doubly distressing at times), but the distinction of orders is still workable and important. When Augustine is pained by tragic theater, it has to be because the spectacle somehow evokes his belief that he has irrevocably lost something or someone of considerable value to him. I say evoke and not cause because it is not the death of the *fictional* character that is causing him the pain. He knows that Virgil's Dido is not a real person and that unreal people do not die. We can assume, then, that in so far as he feels sorrow over Dido, the fiction of her death must be evoking in him the memory of a real loss—some displaced object of grief.

But now we come to the heart of Augustine's problem, the reason why he cannot trust his love of tragic mimesis. Well-directed sympathy is healthy, the sign of a virtuous intelligence; sympathy for fictional characters is a corruption of sympathy and not just a shadow or a copy of the normal affect. Augustine recalls his old delight in the delight of illicit lovers on stage, his agreeable sorrow for their sorrow. "Today," he notes (*conf.* 3.2.3), "I have more compassion for a person who delights in a shameful act than I do for someone who finds it hard to be denied a hobbled pleasure or miss out on a pathetic felicity." His compassion for the one who puts on the show of vice is now greater, in other words, than for the one who wants to watch but misses out. Is he still talking about theater? It is not so easy to tell. Clearly he is marking his distance from a compassion (*misericordia*) that is more virtual than real—the sort that wants to have something to feel bad about. What he now feels for an agent of tragedy or an actor of vice is no longer so blatantly like that. His compassion has become "more authentic" (*verior*), and by this he means that "the sorrow in it does not delight" (*conf.* 3.2.3: *non in ea delectat dolor*).

The reference to non-delighting sorrow—pure grief—is the key to Augustine's apparent lack of interest in the distinction between theater and real life. No doubt there is a terribly real difference between, say, a staged rape and a real one, between the actor who pretends to delight in rape and the psychopath who actually does. But none of this would be news to Augustine, who was as capable as you or I at making the relevant distinction. He was also well aware of the argument that staged immoralities either desensitize their viewers to real immoralities or (worse) actively encourage immoralities by glorifying them. He advances this argument himself, in passing in the *Confessions* (*conf.* 1.16.25) and at much greater length in *City of God* (*civ. Dei* 2.8 f., 4.26, 6.6 f.), where he faults Homer and other pagan writers for inventing gods who misbehave and give bad behavior a good name. But the moralistic critique of fictionalized affects and actions is the superficial one in Augustine; it suggests too easily that bad theater makes for bad people—a critique less of theater than of the stupidity of human desire and our love of imitation.

The deeper truth for Augustine is that we bring to any tragic spectacle a disposition to *weaken* the distinction between suffering people and fictions. It can take extraordinary skill—sometimes on the order of a Virgil or a Homer—to invent the spectacle that supplies our disposition with the verisimilitude it craves. If Dido becomes for us too grievable a character, a fiction no more, then we have a compelling motive to set Virgil aside: for no one willingly embraces a poet who evokes too well the grief that delights not. No human poet, however, can literally make the word flesh and subject the lover of an incarnate life to real bereavement; only God can do that. There is no danger, then, that we can be *absolutely* deceived by a poet's finite powers of verisimilitude, even when that poet is as prodigious as a Virgil. It is clearly possible for us, on the other hand, not to be taken in at all. Fictions that are transparent are notoriously uncompelling; they disappoint. What we want is neither a life confined to our mundane selves nor a life removed entirely from our familiar affections; we want to be both within and outside of ourselves at once, like some spectator to a riveting drama. Practitioners of the dramatic arts— rhetoric included—may choose to exploit this want of ours, but they do not invent the disposition that underwrites it. If the disposition is corrupt, the corruption lies in the spectating. That is the part, Augustine warns us, that deserves less of our compassion.

In a remarkable stretch of the *Confessions* (*conf.* 4.4.7 to 4.7.12), one that is ostensibly Augustine's memorial to a childhood friend of his who dies of fever (a friend he never names), he recounts for us a grief that is as theatrical as it is intense. To say that his grief was theatrical is not to suggest that he was putting on a show of grief, that he felt little of nothing of grief within himself, that he was, all told, only acting. On the contrary, Augustine concedes from his confessional point of view that he was overwhelmed at the time by his friend's death and profoundly disoriented (*conf.* 4.4.9):

> My heart was wholly in grief's shade, and death was whatever I looked at. My native land was a punishment to me; my father's house a strange and luckless place. The things I had shared with my friend turned and tortured me cruelly in his absence. My eyes kept seeking him out everywhere, and he was gone. I hated everything

> because nothing had him; nor could anything still say to me, "look, he is on his way," as when he was alive and just away. I had become a great question to myself.

If there is an element of theater in all this grieving, it comes in the form of Augustine's fascination with his own great question, the question of himself. There is nothing plainly wrong with turning one's life into a question; such a turn is arguably the beginning of all the philosophical virtues. But Augustine's turn to his life's great question is supposed to be the offering of his grief. Having some sense of the good he has lost with the loss of his friend, he lives on to wonder what good yet remains to him—a great question to be sure. Its framing presupposes, however, that Augustine's sorrow over his friend's death is quite unlike his grief for Dido. The sorrow must be without the element of delight in loss, and the friend must be real to him, not a fiction. In fact Augustine gives us good reason to think that the framing of his great question was still that of tragic spectacle. But because he *wants* us to notice the theatricality of his grief and be unmoved by it, his confessional offering is actually a form of anti-tragic theater. If we can begin to notice how his confession works against the seduction of tragic mimesis, we may be less tempted to sympathize with his grief and more likely to feel for his sin.

The hard part will be to feel for his sin. Augustine often speaks as if it were obvious what it means to grieve for a person's moral stupidities and misbegotten affections, but the idea of that kind of grief can easily devolve into a contemptuous pity. It speaks like this: "Really too bad for the wretch so given to vice, so lacking in moral backbone, so clueless about what is of real value in life—I feel sorry for him." Although sentiment of that sort is far from Augustine's core idea of what is grievable about sin, it will take some unearthing to get to the difference. The need for digging has partly to do with the depth of his psychological insights into sin and grief, but more directly it has to do with just how diverting the feeling of contempt can be. There is something hard to resist about the spectacle of someone else's self-defeat; perhaps it conveys to us the hope that even on the way to hell something in us is still in charge. If so, then self-contempt is not going to be less of a lure for a self desperate for self-mastery than contempt of others; it is going to be the mother of that other contempt. Imagine Augustine being able to cast the two parts of his time-fractured self into a perfectly contained scene: his confessing self looks down at his past self, knowing it to be self-defeated, while his past self, still imagining itself a victim, looks for consolation. The knowingness of the confessional self is what turns the scene of an old grief into tragic theater. To leave the theater, Augustine will have to resist self-contempt as best he can and remain open in his confession to an uncharted grief. He hints at that grief, lying quietly beneath the tumult of his distress, when he writes (*conf.* 4.6.11): "I was miserable, as miserable as any soul defeated by its friendship with mortal things; the loss of these things lacerates the soul, and then it feels the misery by which it was miserable even before taking its losses."

The prior misery to which Augustine alludes is the misery of mortality itself, but his words suggest something more than a generalized lament over the mortal condition; they gesture to an original grief, echoed in subsequent griefs, but never fully present there—and so, it would seem, a grief impossible to mourn. Consider: I can, as a mortal being, fear my own death, but I am never in a position to mourn myself; only in my imagination am I at my own funeral. The closest I come to mourning myself is feeling the loss of someone who has entered into my self-definition; I lose a portion of myself, psychologically speaking, when that person is lost to me. In his confession of grief, Augustine adds two thoughts to this brief sketch of my mortal self-awareness. One is that my fear of my own death gives me an incentive not to surrender significant pieces of my self-definition to others (presuming, of course, that I have a choice here); the other is that the loss of a loved one reminds me not of my own death (there is still nothing to remember here) but of my soul's prior separation from God—a grief that is written into the code of my mortal flesh. The first thought is easier to take in, and so let's begin with that one.

By the time Augustine writes the *Confessions*, he will have lost his father, his mother, his son and only child, Adeodatus, and a longtime friend and confidant, Nebridius. And yet the grief he decides to showcase there is for a man whom he hesitates to remember as a friend (*conf.* 4.4.7): "He was not my friend then, and yet when he did become one, it was not really a true friendship—for no friendship is true unless the love poured into our hearts by way of your holy spirit, a gift to us, adds glue to the clinging." Augustine refers to the time when he and this unnamed "friend" (for lack of a better term) were boys together in Thagaste. They weren't so close then, but when Augustine returns to his hometown from his first few years in Carthage, the two reconnect and the affection between them sets off on its short but apparently very sweet run (*conf.* 4.4.7): "You took the man away from this life when scarcely a year had gone by in my friendship, a thing sweet to me above all the sweetness of that life of mine." When the grief comes, it finds Augustine anxious and self-preoccupied. He recalls having had a greater attachment to his wounded self than to his dead friend (*conf.* 4.6.11): "For although I wanted my wretched life to change, I was more unwilling to lose it than lose him, and I don't know whether I would have traded my life for his, as in the story (if not made-up) of Orestes and Pylades, who were willing to die at the same time, each for the other, it being worse than death for them not to live together." He wonders why his grief should have focused him so much on his own death, and for a brief few sentences, he lapses into a false sentimentality. Perhaps he and his friend were two halves of a single soul; with one half gone, Augustine clung to the other—not wishing the whole of his friend to die. This will seem to him, in retrospect, a "light-weight aside" in an otherwise "heavy confession" (*retr.* 2.6.2).

Elsewhere in book 4 he makes it clear that he had very little of his self-definition invested in his friend, certainly far less than half. Around the time of their friendship, Augustine was in the habit of making his close friends into Manichees, this friend being no exception. When his friend lapsed into feverish dementia and was baptized unawares (presumably at the request of his family), Augustine confidently believed that his friend would wake up his old self and be glad to have his near-death baptism mocked as senseless. As it turns out, his friend wasn't so glad. "He was horrified at me," Augustine recalls (*conf.* 4.4.8), "as if I were his enemy, and with an astonishing and sudden sense of independence, he warned me that if I wanted to be his friend, I would have to stop saying such things to him." Augustine's resolve in the face of his friend's unexpected defiance was to wait for a better time to reassert his influence, but that time never comes. His friend dies days later, while Augustine is away (*conf.* 4.4.8): "He was snatched away from my dementia, so that he might be safe with you and a consolation for me." For the confessing Augustine, it was dementia more culpable than a fever that had once made him plot his friend's subversion. But what the confessing Augustine and his unconfessed former self both seem to agree on is this: with the time and the material before him, Augustine was able to shape his friend like so much clay—"I could do what I wanted with him" (*conf.* 4.4.8).

## DEATH AND THE DELINEATION OF SOUL

Augustine's self-portraiture in book 4 of the *Confessions* is designedly narcissistic, and that includes his "light-weight aside," when he reduces his friend's death to a moment in his own dying. The only quality of his friend that seems irreducible to Augustine's ego is his friend's surprising resistance to having his reverences further manipulated. But this is certainly not the quality that the master persuader, in all his noisy mourning, misses. He misses his friend's pliability, and left without a suitable study for his self-image, he leaves Thagaste and returns to Carthage, where he will find other friends, other studies. His old delights return to him over time, and they are attended, he reports, not by "different sorrows" but by "different causes of sorrow" (*conf.* 4.8.13). The characters change, but the story remains depressingly the same—"a long story," he confesses, and "a big lie." The story has him delighting and grieving over friends who move in and out of his life without significantly changing his self-definition; the lie resides in his attempt to define himself in terms of a corrupted reverence. Augustine has taken from the Manichees a license to disown his inner deformities and revere himself as a piece of God. He expects his friends—the other pieces of God—to confirm for him (endlessly) the validity of the license.

But it is not Manicheism that is Augustine's fundamental problem in book 4. There are plenty of bad ways to construe the difference between God and soul, self and other, mind and body and no right way that puts a person in command of those differences. The narcissism to which Augustine is confessing is not the product of an ideology, Manichean or otherwise; it is the default form that reverence takes whenever reverence is made to serve fear. If it were truly possible to live narcissistically—that is, if the reverence in it were not corrupted but just different—it would be possible to reduce all grief to fear of death. Augustine shows us the way. If I grieve for a loved one, then I grieve, narcissistically speaking, solely for a part of myself. I may try to convince myself that I have lost only a self-image and not my true self, closer to me than any image, but this is just the other move in the logic of narcissism—the logic of an all-or-nothing selfhood. For either I exist absolutely (and so play the part of Narcissus), or I fade into nothingness (and play Echo). But Augustine, remember, is *confessing* to narcissism, and no one who is able to confess—to speak *with* another—is constitutionally a narcissist. We should not be so quick, then, to conclude from the theatricality of his grief that he was feeling no grief at all, but only fear of death. The fundamental oneness or unity of love is not for him a narcissist's conceit; it is the divine space in which love is offered and returned (*ex pluribus unum*): "It is this unity," he explains (*conf.* 4.9.14), "that is loved in friends—so much so that we feel guilty if we don't love back the one loving us or if we don't love the one loving us back, looking for nothing more physical in response than signs of good will."

But now we have arrived at the deepest current of Augustine's confession of grief: his belated recognition of his original capacity for love—"Late I loved you, beauty so old and so new; I loved you late" (*conf.* 10.27.38).

## A grievable God

In Luke's parable of the prodigal son (Lk. 15:11–32), the younger of two sons leaves his father's house with his share of the property and travels to a distant country, where he quickly squanders his inheritance through dissolute living. When famine reduces his adopted land to a place of terrible need, the younger son—now with only need to his name—hires himself out to feed someone else's pigs, whose slop he finds himself coveting. Humiliated and desperate, he resolves to return to his father's house, even if that means, as he assumes it must, that he will live out his life as a slave there. His father has other ideas. He sees his son returning from a far distance and, filled with compassion, rushes out to meet him. He will have none of his son's offer to exchange sonship for servitude. Instead the father acts as if his son were back from the dead; he arranges for a great celebration in his honor—greater than the stay-at-home older boy had ever seen or experienced.

Augustine interjects himself into his own version of the prodigal's tale in book 2 of the *Confessions*. The set-up is simple enough. We are back in Thagaste. Augustine is an adolescent, about 16, and he and some other adolescent boys—his usual gang—decide one night to steal some pears from a tree near his family's vineyard. They carry off armfuls of illicit fruit and discard most of what they take as so much pig-food. But their aim was never to savor the pears that were, in any case, "not especially beautiful or tasty." The whole appeal of the exercise, Augustine recalls, was the thrill of transgression itself (*conf.* 2.4.9): "Even if we ate a few, what was pleasing to us was all the same—to do what was not allowed."

There are already some obvious divergences from Luke's parable. Augustine is not wasting an inheritance he has been freely given; he is squandering a fruit he is forbidden by law to take. And not just him: he would not have dared to break the law had he been on his own and less mindful of his need to belong (*conf.* 2.8.16). Augustine weaves into his prodigal's tale two of the elements that he associates with original sin (Gen. 3:6): poverty of motive (there is no good reason to defy God and lose Eden) and a disposition to substitute consensus for a lack of reason (no one loses Eden alone). In so doing, he shifts his focus to the prodigal nature of sin itself—a form of self-willed poverty, veiled as a movement into licentious self-expression.

This focus of his becomes increasingly clear as he delves more deeply into his motive for sinning and finds that he has to discard along the way, like some prodigal analyst, all the obvious candidates: material beauties, sensual pleasures, social perks, power plays. "Sin," he summarizes (*conf.* 2.5.10), "is committed for all these and similar goods when the better and best goods—you, my God, your truth, your law—are deserted on account of an unlimited desire for them, the most limited of goods." He is not explaining to us (or to God) what sin is; he is underscoring sin's fundamental mystery. For here we have a desire whose ambition always mysteriously outstrips its chosen object—as if it were essentially a desire not to be satisfied, a desire for restlessness. Augustine and his adolescent friends may have thought that the fruit of transgression gave them goods to spare. In fact they were confusing divine love (extra-legal and self-offering) with insatiable desire (illicit and self-consuming). The effect of such confusion is, from the hindsight of confession, clear to Augustine (*conf.* 2.10.18): "I slipped away from you in my adolescence and strayed, my God—it was a big detour from your steadiness, and I became to myself a place of desolation" (*regio egestatis*).

But what makes Augustine's account of sin finally so hard to fathom is his tendency to slip between effect and motive. It is sin's effect, he thinks, to sow alienation between his soul, the life of his body, and God, the life of his soul—a split of life from life (*conf.* 3.6.10). Does he also think that this effect, which is a prescription for dying, doubles as a motive? Does his soul sometimes prefer death and the withering of life to life in abundance? "I loved being wrecked," Augustine recalls (*conf.* 2.4.9); "I loved my defection; I loved the defecting in my defection and not something else—my disfigured soul breaking from your firm place into a shambles and craving not some ugly thing but ugliness itself (*dedecus*)." If we remember that the opposite of God for Augustine (the ex-Manichee) is not ugliness but nothing at all, then his soul's desire to become absolutely ugly sounds like a death-wish. But a few sections later he seems to imply that the desire for ugliness is really just a twisted desire for more life (*conf.* 2.6.14). The logic here is prodigal: bad souls get noticed; good souls get ignored. When the prodigal Augustine affects to love particular things (friends, pears) only to discard them for the security of an objectless love, he marks his distance from God, whom he imagines can and does love particular things without fear of loss (*conf.* 2.6.13). At the same time he singles himself out, in his pathetically prodigal way, as one of the things to be loved by God or discarded—perhaps both.

Augustine will compare his adolescent law-breaking to a prisoner's self-assertion. Such asserting takes place within the tightly restricted bounds of an apparent impunity. It is at best "a shadowy imitation of absolute power" (*tenebrosa omnipotentiae similitudine*; *conf.* 2.6.14), but still an imitation. Does the prisoner want to be noticed and risk punishment or be forever left to his tiny domain of self-assertion, which is, in reality, a deceit (*fallacia*)? Augustine is still not sure, looking back, whether a rejection of divine law is ever its own motive. Can a soul really want to reject a law just because it is absolutely a law?

Whatever the significance of Augustine's hesitations about the willfulness of sin (a topic for the next chapter), this much is already fixed in his mind: that the soul cannot be materially human (incarnate) and always have to reckon with the original loss, whether willed or suffered, of its life with God. That conjunction spells prodigality with a vengeance. For what could it mean to gain or lose a life if life itself has already been removed from the picture? The material world, when made to signify mostly God's absence, ends up a ghostly signpost, everything in it pointing to what is not there. Material beloveds make no lasting impression on the prodigal soul; they are just so many disposable reminders of an unsatisfied desire for spirit. Their loss occasions further craving but never real grief.

There is no alternative for Augustine to this pseudo-grief until he begins to reckon with the loss of God *within* the material plane—a grievable loss that (miraculously) leaves something of substance behind. He tries to describe the impact of the human death of God on his human grieving in book 4 of the *Confessions*, a book otherwise preoccupied with the mere trappings of woe (*conf.* 4.12.19):

> He who is our life came down to us, endured our death, and killed it with his own life's abundance: and like thunder, he called us to return to him from here and into that hidden place from which he first came forth to us—the virgin womb. It was there that humanity was wedded to him, mortal flesh, not to be mortal forever. And like a bridegroom from the bridal bed he leapt with joy from there, a giant to run his course. For he did not delay, but ran calling out with his words, actions, death, life, descent, ascent—calling out for us to return to him. He left our sight, so that we might return to our heart and find him there. He went away, and look: here he is.

The passage, with its weave of scriptural motifs (e.g., Jn. 6:33; Ps. 18:6/ New RSV 19:5), is tricky. Augustine tells us that Christ has killed death by dying, but when we look around us, we see quickly that death is alive and well. People still die. How does the death of Jesus Christ, God incarnate, change that basic fact? I take Augustine to mean something like this: I get my life back, a resurrection of sorts, when I stop trying to set the terms for my experience of a loved one's death. It is through the confusion of a loss with the anticipation of a loss that I am constantly willing the death of God and trying to master the imagined world left to me—a disposition that makes me one of Augustine's many prodigals. It is only the actual death of God that can preempt whatever death it is that I have been trying to imagine. All other candidates succumb to fear and the imagination that fear inspires. If Christ is to be other than one more signpost to a blind and fanciful craving for security, his death must be more than the mere representation of a death. It must be real and his own; it cannot be dematerialized and neatly traded in for a sign. "He endured our death" (*tulit mortem nostram*), Augustine writes; in other words, he died. Christ's death is ours in the way that any death is: a thing to be mourned, to be endured. This is not to deny the exceptional nature of his death and the mystery that attends it. But the mystery is not that Christ rises from the dead and renders all death—or perhaps all deaths but one—an illusion; it is that his death somehow makes it possible for other deaths to remain irreducibly particular. The lives that go along with those deaths are likewise particular. They return from an unloved place in the imagination, a place of fear, to a region of loss and renewal, where life is labored and often difficult, but no longer desolate.

I'll conclude with a few thoughts about Augustine's grief over the death of his mother, Monnica, the person who most materially shaped his self-conception. Indeed she appears in the *Confessions* as something of an antithesis to the unnamed friend of book 4, whose self-conception Augustine had done so much to shape—until those startling last few days, which left him reeling in his grief. Whereas Augustine was convinced that he could, given a fighting chance, use his sophisticated intellect to keep his friend Manichean, Monnica had a prophetic confidence that her (overly) sophisticated son would one day abandon his Manichean conceits and return to the faith of his childhood—her faith. She was not inactive in her confidence. She followed him wherever he went, even when he clearly wanted to give her the slip (*conf.* 5.8.15); she shared her dreams with him, which she read as foreclosures of *his* fate (*conf.* 3.11.19–20); she wept through her anxieties for him before bishops, one of whom assured her (with some exasperation) that she would never lose "the son of those tears" (*conf.* 3.12.21); and when her son's moment of truth capped off his bout of pure anguish in a Milanese garden, she was there, just indoors, ready to hear all about his new resolve (*conf.* 8.12.30).

Augustine professes to have had mostly gratitude for the "great solace" that Monnica gave him in life (*conf.* 9.12.30), but he was not wholly without misgiving as to the depth of her influence on him, right down to his core identity. The telling incident for him comes early (*conf.* 4.11.17–18). He seemed to be dying of chest pain and fever while still a small boy, and believing what his mother believed about salvation, he begged her for the sin-cleansing sacrament of baptism. She hastily made the necessary arrangements for the ritual, fearing his death was imminent. But when his fever suddenly broke, she postponed his baptism on the supposition that her son's adolescent transgressions were still ahead of him and would be less grievously reckoned to his unbaptized soul. Augustine, looking back, clearly would have preferred a path of less solicited transgression, even if that were to have risked sins of greater gravity. His mother seemed at the time to trust her sense of her son's psychology more than the efficacy of the sacrament and the care of the Church. The hard part about that for him, one may venture to suppose, is that she was right about his psychology.

If sin's narcissistic logic of all-or-none selfhood *just is* the logic of love, then we have no more reason to believe in Augustine's grief for his mother than in his grief for his unnamed friend; in both cases, a projective identification of the griever with the grieved—in one case self-aggrandizing ("you are me"), in the other self-effacing ("I am you")—will have resolved his grief back into fear of death. But to speak of grief this way is already to suggest that grief exists prior to its narcissistic reduction and that the love in true grief is sinless. Augustine describes getting a foretaste of this original love, while in his mother's company, about a week before her death. I refer to his famous description of his joint vision with her at Ostia, their port of departure from Rome (*conf.* 9.10.23–25). At the time of the vision the two of them are looking out upon a garden at the house where they were staying while waiting to go home; they talk intimately with one another about what the eternal life of the saints must be like. Soon they find themselves in an altered state, no longer connected to the things of this perishable world; they are taken up into the intimacy of the unmediated Word, timeless and yet time-producing. Augustine's conversation with his mother continues even there, where both hear with their minds, not their ears (*conf.* 9.10.25): "Now we stretch forth and in a blink of cognition (*rapida cogitatione*) touch upon the eternal wisdom that abides above all things."

The visionary part of this vision is not of eternal wisdom—that is imageless—but of a mother and a son. Monnica in the vision is still Monnica, and Augustine is still Augustine. There is no evidence of dematerialization in this original state of things. Mother and son do not merge into a single soul, nor do they sink into the abyss of God. They talk with one another, even as the Word hovers eternally over their breakable speech. Perhaps there is reason to think, if the vision can be trusted, that being born of a woman is not a natural cause of love's degeneration into something unlovable and not worth grieving. If the Word can itself be born of a woman, then there is no reason not to trust the vision. The grief that Augustine feels, or fails to, does depend after all on a grievable God.

## CHAPTER TWO

# SIN AND THE INVENTION OF WILL

*The work of the eye is complete now;*
*work next at the heart's work—*
*on those images you've captured within you,*
*led in and overcome and left unknown.*
*Look—inside bridegroom—on your inside bride,*
*so superbly drawn out of a thousand natures:*
*a beauty thus far won,*
*but thus far never loved.*
                    Rainer Rilke (trans. William Gass)

There are two places in Augustine's theology where the will appears to be absolute, and by absolute I mean loosed from a sufficiently motivating good and left to its own devices. One place is sin; the human will to sin is always unaccountably perverse. The other place is grace; the divine will to save is always generous beyond reckoning. Let's begin with sin.

Suppose that I lie for the sake of a friendship and that my lie is a sin (as is any lie for Augustine; see *mend.* 9–24). In keeping with the characterization of sin that he advances in book 2 of his *Confessions* (*conf.* 2.5.10), it may be true that I would not have lied were I not trying to preserve a friendship ("no, really, I love it when you bring your kids to visit"), but no friendship could ever move me *all* the way to sin. Sinful desire is, by virtue of being sinful, poorly defined and lacking in proper measure; it is desire that is always out of kilter with the desirability of its object.

In the first book of *On Free Will*, written while Augustine was still in Rome and in a decidedly anti-Manichean mood, he characterizes sin as an unaccountable preference for temporal over eternal goods (*lib. arb.* 1.15.31 to 1.16.34). Temporal goods are mundane things like money, health, and citizenship; eternal goods are mighty abstractions like God, Truth, and Law. Forget for a moment what it would mean for a temporal being to love mainly the things of eternity. Augustine's point is that temporal goods are naturally limited in value; these are the goods that can and will be lost involuntarily. If I deliberately value a good as fragile and time-mortgaged as a friendship over something as substantial and unchanging as the truth, then I am reading a value into things—an eternal value—that is just not there. It is not my mind, Augustine tells me, that initiates this kind of eisegesis, but my will. "Nothing but the will," he writes (*lib. arb.* 1.16.34), "can depose the mind from its original place of authority and proper order" (*de arce dominandi rectoque ordine*).

Now let's turn to grace. It is not clear how Augustine's God can will to love temporal things, like people, and avoid sin's kind of eccentricity, where wisdom and resolve fall out of alignment. The issue here is not whether God can be conceived to have a reasonable basis for preferring some people over others. It has been a stable feature of Augustine's doctrine of election, going back to the beginning of his episcopacy (*Simpl.* 1.2; cf. *retr.* 2.1), that divine favor is never merited. The selective advantages that might have allowed some individuals to stand out and earn their place among the saints are, in Augustine's reading, all divine gifts. If I embody a virtue that you do not have or come nearer to perfecting a virtue that is for you an ill fit, I bear witness in my person to the workings of divine spirit; I do not earn a claim to superior merit. My actions may sometimes be more laudable than yours and vice versa, but as for the worth of our respective persons, only God, "on the basis of some kind of hidden equity, humanly unfathomable" (*Simpl.* 1.2.16), can judge.

However morally unsettling this doctrine of election may seem, it distracts from the more basic issue of what an original grace is. Suppose that there is a prior kind of goodness that can render some people more worthy of divine favor than others. And let's be as benignly Pelagian as possible about this. You have certain natural gifts—a quick and flexible mind, an unaffected affability, and a gentle sense of humor; you also have certain natural liabilities—a disposition to debilitating self-doubt and a tendency to overindulge your appetites. You resolve to enhance your gifts and minimize your liabilities in the company of other self-improvers, all of whom have a well-developed social conscience. You and the other members of your dedicated community—your church—constantly encourage and check one another, and over a period of years, you claim for yourself an appropriate and hard-won measure of self-approbation. You do not claim that you have made yourself worthy of God's grace; you simply believe that you made yourself better than you once were, and you gratefully concede the help and support that you have received along the way. This should seem (I hope) a plausible and even pleasing picture of a value-added life.

But now imagine the superabundantly good and perfectly self-communicative God being moved to notice the separate goodness of our human flickers of reflected divine light—and we are still supposing here that we have been able *to enhance* the reflection. It is natural to assume that what there is for God to notice is not separate light (there is no seam within light) but the human will to enhance the light's intensity—an initiative to add good to good. What would such a will look like? Metaphorically speaking, it would be a form of darkness, in that God is lacking, but a pregnant form of darkness, in that God is wanted. The God who sees and acknowledges the separate goodness of this will is able to read darkness into the light of creation without having to break up the created order into light and darkness (the fractured universe of the Manichees). This is a miraculous kind of eisegesis, to be sure, if conceivable at all. Augustine will tend to conceive of it in psychological terms. God interjects desire for God deeply into the soul and then alters the soul's environment of choice in order to elicit, develop, and ultimately to satisfy that desire. Recall the great words (*conf.* 1.1.1): "You stir us and we delight to praise you, who made us yours—and so the heart within us is restless until it rests in you." Augustine will sometimes emphasize exterior prompting (*Simpl.* 1.2.13), at other times interior conception (*gr. et pecc. or.* 1.13.14). Whatever his occasional emphasis, he always brings his psychology of grace back to Paul's pair of questions in First Corinthians (1 Cor. 4:7): "What do you have that you have not received? And if you have received, why boast as if you had not?" The presumptive answers—"nothing at all" and "I really have no reason to boast"—leave the soul beholden but not bereft.

The distinction is crucial. If the soul claims its divine inheritance—its desire for God—for itself alone, a private good, then it lives out the part of the prodigal's tale where the son divests himself of all his wealth, loses his self-worth, and envisions his return to his father's house as a route to enslavement, albeit a slavery preferable to self-willed poverty. If, on the other hand, the soul comes to see that its inheritance is both received and still with God—a receiving that has never annulled the giver (or, for that matter, the receiver's indebtedness)—then we are at the part of the prodigal's tale where the father sees his son returning from a distance, rushes out to meet him, and reassures him before they return together that he has never been other than a much loved son to his father. Self-willed poverty not only does not diminish that original love; it sets the stage for its entrance into a human consciousness. Consider that the son is still in his wasteland, his "place of desolation" (*regio egestatis*; *conf.* 2.10.18), when his father comes calling.

What is it about the soul that makes it want to lose love in order to regain it? This is what Augustine wonders (*conf.* 8.3.7). More than that, he wonders what makes his divine father so favorably disposed to resurrections (*conf.* 8.3.6). The father in Luke's parable had only this to say to his perplexed and angry *other* son, the one who put such stock in holding fast and never dying (Lk. 15:31–32): "Son, you are always with me, and all that is mine is yours. But we had to celebrate and rejoice—this brother of yours was dead and has come to life; he was lost and now is found." The words explain nothing. They simply invite the older brother to be his brother's keeper and receive the love he feels has been denied him: "all that is mine is yours." It would take a certain kind of prodigality to be able to accept such an invitation, a give-away of self-definition. The older brother in Luke and Augustine's Pelagian both count on the self-definition of a virtuous life; theirs is a virtue-first selfhood. They cannot accept the love that preempts their virtues without undoing themselves. But they are not being asked to accept; they are being prompted to remember. And when they begin to recall that they are themselves the prodigals they disdain, being creatures of change, they will also need to remember what never changes. Augustine accents the note of stability in his gloss of the prodigal's eternal father (*conf.* 8.3.6): "You are always the same, and the things that are not always the same you always know in your same way."

It is tempting to imagine something very abstracted, almost wholly spectral here: we have the divine father who is at one with his own knowing but who is alien to the dying things known to him. He just looks out from the eternal side of his window onto time, change, and loss and never leaves the house. But how can this be the God who sees his time-tried children from a distance and descends to meet them where they stand, even when they are hell-bent on being somewhere else? Augustine's descending God introduces what seems to be contrary motion into the appetite for life, motion that is mimicked or parodied by the sinful soul: a superabundant being moves into the poverty of time; a needy but self-aware being moves into the greater poverty of sin. All this is going to be unaccountable and a check against philosophy if self-diminishment is being willed as an end in itself and not as a nod, however veiled, to some kind of vitality—a changing constant.

When Augustine was a Manichee and still worshipping at the altar of a limited being, he was not thinking that the God of light willed to have his light darkened or that God of darkness, covetous of light, willed to be so needy. This was just how things were. When he reads some of the books of the Platonists (*libri Platonicorum*; *conf.* 7.9.13) and imagines himself decisively freed from his old and much frayed piety, he begins to underscore the willfulness of his soul's alienation from God—as if his God were to have created everything about him but his will to sin. But this is not obviously (or even consistently) a Platonist way of thinking. Plotinus, the great third-century Platonist and a mind much admired by Augustine (*c. Acad.* 3.18.41), associates evil (κακόν) with free-form want and disorder and denies that we have it within us to initiate true chaos (*enn.* 1.8.5): "We cannot be, ourselves, the source of Evil, we are not evil in ourselves; Evil was before we came to be; the Evil which holds human beings down binds them against their will."

In this chapter I want to look more carefully at absoluteness of will in Augustine. I especially want to test the connection in his thought between will and spirit—a conjunction that speaks to his Platonism. He gets from the Platonists, Plotinus especially, a philosophical idiom for articulating the distinction between the richly knowable world where God dwells (the father's country, the *patria*) and the world of scarcity and struggle, a construct of sin and the senses, where God's presence is either overlooked or withdrawn (the distant country of the prodigal, the *saeculum*). For Augustine's purposes, the most important thing ever to have happened in the history of philosophy is Plato's discovery of the difference between an intellected world (*mundus intellegibilis*) and a sensed one (*mundus sensibilis*)—a discovery he passes along to the school of philosophy he founds: the Academy. After Plato, Christians would have a way of joining with philosophers in a mutual disdain for the wisdom of this (sensed and sinful) world—"the philosophy that our sacred writings quite rightly despise" (*c. Acad.* 3.19.42).

In his critique of the Academics, the first work of his post-conversion philosophy (and so written shortly after November of 386), Augustine tries to beat back the skeptical turn of the Academic tradition—taken, he thinks, in reaction to Stoic materialism—and convince his Christian auditors that knowledge, or the return to the epistemic equivalent of God's country, is at least possible. Near the end of his meandering display of philosophical hope, Augustine advances the unexpected thesis that the Academics never believed in their own skepticism; they were merely trying to dissuade others from adopting a conception of knowledge that was restricted to bodies and bound to be deceived even about them (*c. Acad.* 3.17.38 to 3.20.43). The more seasoned Academics revealed the heart of Platonism—its dogma of the two worlds—only to mentally purified insiders.

As a historical thesis about the inner workings of the Academy, Augustine's posit of an esoteric tradition is at best slimly supported conjecture, but as an expression of his own sense of the limits of disputation, his posit speaks worlds. Of course his Platonists would lack the argumentative means to call the most sophisticated materialists of their day—the Stoics—back home. The Stoics were like any others whose thoughts wander the world of sin and sensibilia, a truth-like world but not true (*illum uerum, hunc ueri similem*; *c. Acad.* 3.17.37): they may be led to notice the poverty of their situation by way of the limited and wholly negative offering of skepticism, but no argument could be expected to convert their poverty to wealth.

Fundamentally for Augustine we do not arrive at truth; the truth arrives at us and embraces us in our place of bodily internment. The result is less the satisfaction of our desire to live secure in the truth than its humanization. Augustine adds to Platonism the irony of an intelligence that has become in its self-offering more human than most humans have been willing to be. Apart from the power of that irony to reshape a consciousness, there is no escape for us from the truth-like world of appetite and imagination and into something real; there is no Platonism (*c. Acad.* 3.19.42):

> This philosophy [Platonism] is not the philosophy of this world—the philosophy that our sacred writings quite rightly despise, but of the other world, the intelligible one. But the most refined kind of reasoning would never recall souls there who have been blinded

by the multiform darkness of error and dulled by the meanest kind of corporality—not unless God on high, out of a kind of general clemency, were to bend and lower the source of divine intellect to the level of a human body. Stirred not only by commands but also by things done, souls could collect themselves and regain their sense of their father's country, even without an arsenal of arguments.

Augustine does not say that arguments in philosophy are useless, but he implies that they are not very useful apart from the shock of a prior recognition. The recognition has something to do with how achingly open the desire for wisdom must remain in a context of a human life, where divinity touches down but never rests; the shock comes with seeing how easy it has been to serve a childlike form of this desire, more given to appetite and imagination, and to resist the beauty of its development.

So far all of this is more or less in line with Plato, whose Socrates—the paradigmatic teacher of philosophy—has an uncanny sense of the divine possibilities of an open desire for wisdom and of the awful cost of fixing the form of that desire prematurely. But where Plato is not making Socrates out to be the personification of divine eros (despite a few hints to the contrary in the *Symposium*), Augustine's Jesus expresses in his person the perfect intimacy between infinite wisdom and open desire. And open is what a finite desire for infinite wisdom has to be. The satisfaction of such desire—and so the end of a life of prodigal longing—does not, however, have to cost us our humanity, not if God, while still being fully God, has been able to live with his. Again the truth of the incarnation is, for Augustine, never vouchsafed through argument; either that peculiar Advent has already entered into philosophical memory, or philosophy is a name for aimless wandering in a foreign land.

Augustine's thickly Christological qualification of philosophical possibility is apt to seem anti-philosophical to all but the most self-surrendering types. Although I do not share that impression myself, I want to give it its due. How can a fact as peculiar and particular as the conjoining of the eternal Logos to a first-century Nazarene rabbi possibly matter to the history of philosophy? Note that I say fact and not idea. If the particular *fact* of the incarnation makes all the difference, then the Platonists who live before Christ have no hope of sharing in the form of intelligence that they have so oddly been able to describe. If it is the idea that matters, then in theory at least those same Platonists may have found some way, other than having to be reborn in Christian times, to get to the idea that the two worlds are really one in God's logic: hence the Word made flesh.

Augustine sometimes talks as if Christianity—the Christ-event and the historical church—were the authoritative means by which whole peoples could come to resist the love of temporal things and know (eventually) what a few Platonists once knew to be spirit. As he puts it in *On True Religion*, a Platonist-friendly early work (*c.* 390; *vera rel.* 4.6), Christianity emerged to close the gap between "the timid guesses of the few" and "the manifest correction and redemption of multitudes." If the implication is that the old Platonists had the right knowledge but no means of conveying it effectively, even to themselves, then Augustine's qualified praise of Platonic foresight is puzzling, to say the least. It is like the prodigal son praising his older brother for his keen prior knowledge of their father's house. Nothing about that knowledge would have kept the prodigal from leaving. At the time he knew as much about his father's love for him as his older brother did—and as little.

The alternative reading has Augustine sensing illusion in Platonist claims to knowing—the illusion that they have managed more than a gifted guess at higher things. They get appropriately disillusioned (if they do) in the same manner that anyone does: divine reality intrudes. Augustine's Christian Platonists, who confuse love of the higher with disdain for the lower, are no less burdened with illusion. They are just promoting a different form of it. I resort again to the prodigal's tale. The old Platonists, calling themselves pagans, make the older brother's mistake: they claim knowledge of (spiritual) wealth. The new Platonists, calling themselves Christians, make the younger brother's mistake: they presume to know what (spiritual) poverty is. Neither brother has reckoned yet with the unsettling generosity of their father—a generosity they have scarcely been able to imagine. When it hits them, they will have to reckon not only with their own illusions but also with one another's. There is an intimate relationship in Augustine's mind between Platonism and Christianity, but neither of these soul-maps has the power to describe for him more than places in his imagination—unless God decides otherwise and wrecks what has proved to be an imaginary integrity.

When Augustine describes his own reception of Platonism in book 7 of the *Confessions*, he seems at first to be describing his initiation into the knowledge of divine wealth, to be followed all too quickly by his return to familiar, God-bereft poverty. Such an impression encourages the reading—a commonplace in the scholarship—that leaves Augustine Platonist in his mind but Christian in his resolve; he supposedly gets help from the incarnate God to disdain the world of bodies and begin his road home to an immaterial paradise. The chief failing of this reading is that it makes Platonism into what it can never be for Augustine: a solution, if even only a partial one, to the problem of sin. That problem is not primarily a lack of knowledge but a presumption of it—a willful ignorance. In book 7 Augustine struggles with his temptation to believe that he been given, through Platonism, his insider's glimpse of his father's wealth (older brother's knowledge) and that he has generated, through his own sin, his outsider's grip on poverty (younger brother's knowledge). It is only in book 8, where he yields to a directive to put on Christ and look no longer to lusts to care for his flesh (Rom. 13:13–14; *conf.* 8.12.29), that he finally sees his two-faced temptation for what it is: a temptation.

At the end of book 7 Augustine is at that place in his knowledge of God where his Platonists of old once were in theirs: he seems to know before he knows—a knowledge B.C., even though Augustine lives, in the most obvious of ways, "in Christian times" (*tempora Christiana*). Christ has lived and died, and "there can be no doubt," he says (*vera rel.* 3.3), "as to which religion should be held above the rest." He also claims that the old Platonists—Plato and the rest of them—would have been Christian in Christian times, "with the change of a few words and a few sentiments" (*vera rel.* 4.7). But Augustine's Platonism does not make *him* a Christian, and it is here, at the strange disjuncture between philosophy and reverence, that the difference between Platonism old and new ceases to matter very much. For it is not Platonism, minus Christ, that supplies Augustine with his most tempting illusion of a disincarnate knowledge; it is his own will that has supplied him with that, under a pretense of absoluteness. Or so I will try to explain.

## PATHOS OF WILL

### Place of unlikeness

His long adolescence—"unspeakably bad" (*conf.* 7.1.1)—behind him, Augustine enters into his thirties feeling mentally blocked. His best philosophical intuition keeps him firmly convinced that something incorruptible and so incapable of losing any of its value is essentially better off than something more vulnerable. But his imagination for incorruptible being remains, to his shame, still stubbornly materialist— a hang-over, he surmises, from his Manichean days. It is not that he thinks of God as an outsized human being, with eternally perfected body parts, but the subtlest alternative he can muster has God playing the part of a boundless cosmic sea, into which the sponge that is everything else, big but finitely big, has been thrown (*conf.* 7.5.7): "from all sides and in every part the sponge was filled by the immense sea." The problem here is that Augustine's matter-bound imagination is blocking him from being able to conceive of his relationship to an incorruptible source of value.

Try to think for a moment in crudely materialist terms about value (it is not as easy as it may seem at first). Take materialism to be the thesis that matter is all there is. The materialist God, a being of perfect and inviolate goodness, must be possessed of a certain kind of material perfection. Ignore for now the question of whether a materialist perspective admits of the idea of a particular *kind* of thing—as opposed to a brute, unclassifiable particularity. Ignore whether it admits of ideas at all. The thing to notice is that this God cannot, by nature, undergo material additions or subtractions. If he were to do so, this necessarily self-confined father-figure would become more or less valuable than he already is at present—a sign of imperfection. Augustine hears in this kind of reasoning a decisive refutation of Manichean materialism. The Manichees posit a form of materiality that is not God's. They refer to this matter, says Augustine, as a "race of darkness" (*gens tenebrarum: conf.* 7.2.3). Darkness can sometimes connote evil or what is absolutely other to God, but here such God-bereft otherness is simply a function of material differentiation. I cannot be parted from a source of materialist value without lessening the source. The God of the Manichees suffers diminution merely by virtue of having company. Augustine protests that so delicate a deity can hardly be God. The real God, incorruptible by nature, must somehow be less material and more substantial.

Materialism fails Augustine less because it overvalues matter than because it lacks the internal resources for expressing non-alienating difference. Really all difference is at bottom non-alienating. Absolutely alien things would have nothing in common and so no basis of differentiation, not even thinghood. When two things are intelligibly different, they are also always, in some way, the same kind of thing. The relevant sameness varies with context. Augustine and Alypius are two different men; Augustine and Monnica two different human beings; Augustine and his dog Rex (if he had a dog Rex) two different animals. Materiality may be doing most of the work of differentiation within a kind (the body count), but as the kind is capable of being at more than one place at the same time (usually a deal-breaker for something material), it is not unreasonable to think that material differentiation is a matter of more than mere matter. Naturally I am not trying to foreshorten, in a few short sentences, the great late-modern quest for a materialist account of concepts and concept-acquisition; I am simply pointing out that materialism, as Augustine has come to know it, suffers from an inner poverty. Once he gets over the idea that the Manichees have used it to define a workable difference between God and evil, he finds himself losing his hold on that difference altogether.

His initial inclination is to move in the direction of differentiated will. God, who *is* the good, *wills* only the good; the human being, derivatively good and created in God's image, has a choice: either will the good or will its undoing (God's absence). "It was my intent to look into what I kept hearing," Augustine recalls (*conf.* 7.3.5), "that the cause of our wrongdoing and our being subject to your just judgment is the free choice of the will—but this was a cause I failed to see limpidly." The obscurity to which he confesses has to do with his lack of a good answer to this question: how is it that the divine and the divinely created will can have very different forms of expression—as different as good is from evil? If it had been clear to Augustine at the time that the will (*voluntas*) owes nothing to matter for its expression (i.e., that the will is an immaterial agent), then he might have been moved to invoke the will itself as the determiner of good and evil, a move that would have utterly devalued materiality. But it was not so clear to him, prior at least to his reception of Platonism, how expressions of will could be other than the effects of material forces. And given the will's essential materiality, the boundlessly material divine being (boundless, so to speak, "on all sides") would surely have incorporated within itself all possibilities of will: Augustine's, the devil's, anyone's. Whatever the appearance of independent action, the bounded actor will have been expressing a materiality none other than God's own. "These thoughts," Augustine confesses (*conf.* 7.3.5), "were weighing me down once again, and I could barely breathe."

## SIN AND THE INVENTION OF WILL

Early in the summer of 386, a season or so before he finds his feet with Jesus, Augustine gets either a gift or a loan of books—Platonic writings, all translated from Greek into Latin—from a man he never names, but whom he describes as a big windbag, distended with pride (*immanissimo typho turgidum*; *conf.* 7.9.13). The effect of these books on Augustine's self-conception is little short of momentous. He heeds their directive to him to move into his inner depths (*mea intima*) and see things from an insider's point of view. With God as his guide (*duce te*), he soon arrives at inner illumination—light for the soul's eye—but just as quickly he is snatched away and taken up into a place of unlikeness (*regio dissimilitudinis*; *conf.* 7.10.16), where he hears his creator from afar and sees all the other things (*cetera*; *conf.* 7.11.17), the stuff of creation, below. His point of view, elevated but not ultimate, proves to be mostly unsettling (unlike anything familiar), but the ex-Manichee does emerge from the experience roused from the doldrums of skepticism and made aware of the truth of spirit, "seen and understood by way of things made" (*conf.* 7.10.16; Rom. 1:20).

Does he come away, then, with a new spiritual conception of himself, freed from his material self-image and ready to be judged—spirit before spirit—by the God of commanding will? I doubt it. Given his fuller description of his view from unlikeness, noting particularly his way into that view and his way out, Augustine seems to have been released from a fiction of selfhood, but without being issued new spiritual credentials. His God has used the books of certain Platonists—mostly Plotinus, perhaps some Porphyry—as a Trojan horse into his psyche: a gift of Greek wisdom, normally an incentive to pride of spirit, here humbles the recipient and checks his pride. Admittedly the humbled Augustine does not appear to spare the Platonists his critique of *their* pride; although they presume to know a great deal about spiritual matters, they still know nothing, he submits, about the essential humility of spirit and God's astounding, even disconcerting, love of mortal flesh. But all this is best taken from him as self-indictment (*conf.* 7.19.25): "As for the mystery held in the Word made flesh, I was incapable of even a guess." Augustine, in confession, is the very Platonist he is critiquing.

At the summit of his Platonist presumption, where he sees himself well lit and really loving the good God, not some figment, Augustine is disposed to believe that only his sexual habit (*consuetudo carnalis*; *conf.* 7.17.23)—that witless drive of his to bond with flesh—can call him back into the cave of ignorance. And when his lower self, as he understands it, does come calling, it drags him weak as a baby from his rapture and rejoins him to his carnal attachments. Once again he will face old temptations: about flesh, about spirit, about what he thinks he knows about the two and when he thinks he knows it. But this time he is fortified, not with the question that he has made of himself, but with the question that God has made him to be—the question within the question. The Augustine that we meet in book 7 of the *Confessions* has had his place of inner poverty (*regio egestatis*; *conf.* 2.10.18) transformed into a foreign country, a land of unlikeness. He is being invited to give up his recognition of this place.

Consider his initiation into unfamiliarity. I refer not to his studied retreat to the inmost precincts of his psyche, but to what he speaks of as an involuntary assumption: "When I first learned of you," he tells God (*conf.* 7.10.16), "you raised me up so that I might see the reality of what I was seeing and that I, who was seeing, was not yet real." Dissimilitude is of the very essence of such a perspective. Augustine is being shown, among other things, that he has yet to exist; surely he would have to become unlike himself, an existing being, to take in that truth. But why would he want to take it in? It is a truth that seems to offer him only privation and his life's undoing, a trade of the solid now of his existence for some shadowy not yet. The words that he first hears from his far-off God, calling to him in his unlikely place, seem far from reassuring (*conf.* 7.10.16): "I am the food of grown-ups; grow and you will feed on me. You will not change me into you, as you do the food of your flesh, but you will be changed into me."

Augustine has a strange reaction to hearing these words. He begins to think that this voice without a body, the voice of truth itself (*veritas*), is no less real for being bodiless. Perhaps he prefers, understandably enough, to push back the thought of being materially absorbed into God, like some piece of digestible matter. More tellingly this kind of thought (crudely materialist) is giving way in him to a new kind of thought: that his soul's distention, its stretch into unlikeness, is as much about self-exile as it is about a flesh-bound life. The God who helps him sort out the difference is not the one who gives him his alternative to his material existence; it is the one who abides with him even while he refuses to abide with himself. When Augustine hears that being name itself—"I am who I am" (*conf.* 7.10.16; Exod. 3:14)— his doubts about the sweep of God's existence, the full scope of it, disappear. This is the God who can lead selves out of exile, return them to himself, and remain throughout it all eternally self-consistent. Augustine now knows that material otherness, or what turns out to be the created order, is no place of exile for God (*conf.* 7.10.16; Rom. 1:20): "I would sooner have doubted I was alive than doubt the truth that is seen and understood by way of things made."

When Augustine offers his commentary on the things made, he underscores two aspects of what he sees: the corruptibility and the beauty. Things are corruptible and so liable to lose the beauty of their being just by virtue of not being God: "I surveyed the things below you," he writes (*conf.* 7.11.17), "and I saw that they do not wholly exist nor wholly not exist—they exist, being from you, but they do not exist, not being you." All of the things that are not God are, in a sense, naturally unlike themselves, a mix of nil and being. But taken together, Augustine observes, they can be seen to compose a whole universe—a thing of perfect beauty. "There is simply no evil for you," he tells God (*conf.* 7.13.19), "and not only for you, but for the world of your creation; for nothing is able to break in from the outside and wreck the order you have set in place."

When he moves from corruptible things to the beauty of the whole, Augustine seems to forget that he has been describing corruptibility as an internal matter, the not-being-God liability: the whole of creation, not being God, should be as close to non-being as any of its parts. If it is not, then this can be only because God, as the ultimate imposer of order, has lent stability to the whole that he has not lent to the parts. They too can be beautiful for a time, but their temporary beauty is always a subordinate matter, a nod to the stable whole. Having seen the whole, Augustine is ready to adopt the way of thinking I have just described. Here are his words (*conf.* 7.13.19): "I was no longer wishing for better things, now that I was thinking of all things together—not that superior things aren't still better than inferior ones, but I was holding myself to a healthier judgment: that the good of the whole is better than the best part." The logic of valuation here is less strange than the vision motivating its application. And in this case, it is going to be more illuminating to bring out the strangeness than to follow the logic.

Suppose I try to fit myself into Augustine's vision of a perfected creation. I am, like anything else, somewhere in the *et cetera* of existence—in the sum of things that can be added to God. If there is a summary vision to be had of this sum, I ought to be in it. My first problem of placement is that I have little or no conception of the displaced self (supposedly me) that is looking for itself (still me) in the order of things. I have had one birth; I expect to have one death. What is it that can distance me from my particular birth and death and still somehow leave me with me? I fashion the *idea* of myself. I can imagine this idea playing itself out in a material life, perhaps more than one. Even so, I am not the idea of me. I am me. And it is my stubborn materiality that is going to give me my quickest sense of being a whole unto myself. (Here I withhold judgment about how trustworthy this sense is.)

My second problem of placement begins to loom. How can I be *part* of an alien beauty? Of course I can conceive of beauty that is not my own. I have found that this is the great thing about beauty: that it is not all mine. I can be inspired by its difference and released for a time from having to attend so myopically to the necessities of my self-conception. Indeed I cannot even see my own beauty until it gets refracted and rendered alien to me through the regard of others. They see my beauty as different; I see it through them as different. If my primary relation to beauty is to be that of a part to a whole, then I lose the material difference that opens me to the otherness of beauty and thereby to its inspiration. If I have any hope of seeing the beauty of Augustine's perfected whole of a creation, then I must be on the outside looking in; I cannot be a part of what I see. I have no material place, then, in his idea of creation; if I try to inhabit a place, I disappear into an idea (the idea he presumes to be God's).

Perhaps that is an insight. Plotinus tried to remind us that soul does not translate into matter—at least not the higher or best part of soul (see especially *enn.* 4.8, his tractate on the soul's descent). The best part never descends into time and space and so remains untouched by the materiality that we commonly confuse with the body. True materiality (ὕλη), for Plotinus, is truth's inner antithesis. It is not, as some Manichee might be inclined to think, the gross opposite of truth (dark and heavy stuff as opposed to light); it is the paradoxical place where truth becomes unlike itself. Plotinus has a name for the paradox. He calls it, picking up on a similar notion in Plato (*Politicus* 273 D6–E1), a "place of unlikeness" (τόπος τῆς ἀνομοιότητος; *enn.* 1.8.13). Here is where some part of soul, clearly not the best part, descends to order absolute disorder—a fool's errand. Again the body is not at the root of the seduction; the body is what the soul creates and inhabits in an effort to bring form and beauty to chaos (*enn.* 4.8.5). It is the chaos and its eternal tease of new order that seduces. The philosophical life, when set against this tease, gets styled as the higher soul's attempt to pierce through its needy material persona and prompt ecstatic recollection. The adept of Plotinian philosophy comes to self-identify with soul alone and no longer with some hybrid of spirit and matter (*enn.* 1.4.14). Put otherwise: the soul, having passed through unlikeness, gladly returns to itself and its spiritual home in the One—"the passing of solitary to solitary" (*enn.* 6.9.11).

It is tempting, given Augustine's focus on ecstatic knowledge in book 7, to superimpose a Plotinian itinerary on his findings. But the fit is awkward. Yes he does discover that God is not defined, as a body is, by time and space, and yes this certainly avails his theology of a rich vein of Platonist speculation about spirit. On the other hand, he makes this discovery while in a place of unlikeness. And while it is quite likely that he lifts the term, *regio dissimilitudinis*, from his Latin translation of Plotinus, it is not at all clear that he uses the term with a Plotinian intonation. When Plotinus speaks of the soul's movement into place of unlikeness, he is referring to the soul's tendency (unaccountably perverse) to identify with the chaos that it is otherwise disposed to order. If the identification were ever to be total (and this may be describing an impossibility), soul would no longer be soul but something wholly material—a condition of soul-death. There is reason to think that Augustine views the desire behind sin similarly (it is soul-suicidal desire), but in terms of what he overtly describes in book 7, it is not sin that puts him into his place of unlikeness; *his God has done that*—and without asking. Unlikeness in this case is a given and even an original condition of Augustine's soul. He is being reminded that he is unlike God. A reminder of that sort cannot be a form of knowing for Plotinus, who expects only falsity from unlikeness, never truth (*enn.* 1.8.1). And so where Plotinus is looking to leave his place of unlikeness, Augustine is seeking a way to live in his. It is, after all, *from* a place of unlikeness that Augustine comes to know how profoundly he already loves truth. He has no conceivable reason to want to leave.

The departure he describes is involuntary (*conf.* 7.17.23): "I was not stably fixed in my delight of you, God: I got swept up to your beauty and then soon I was torn away from you by my weight; I crashed into lower things (*in ista*) and groaned—that weight, it was my sexual habit." In his description, he does not specify very precisely what the lower things are. His Latin phrase, *in ista,* conveys a sneer, contempt for the familiar: ugh, *those* things again. Given that they are the objects of Augustine's sexual habit, I assume that you can imagine as well as I what manner of object they may be. It is strange to him, of course, and humiliating, that his bodily desire— his desire, in fact, *for* a body—can outweigh his love of God. He will want to return to his old philosophical intuition, about the superiority of the incorruptible beloved, and add a Platonist gloss. None of this, however, will help him. He will only be further encouraged to think that he has the power to will his unlikeness to God and that his descent into a sexual history has somehow, deep down, been his choice to make.

Augustine knows that he has no good answer to the questions that emerge out of the blind spot in his self-knowledge: why chase after the lesser beauty, why desire a diminished good? Plotinus certainly cannot tell him why a part of his soul (a part?) breaks from soul and develops a taste for material chaos and self-undoing. To seek the answer in some stupid pride (*superbia*; *civ. Dei* 12.6) or in a reckless daring (τόλμα; *enn.* 4.8.5) is to paste a label on an incoherence: for what gives birth to a dark and perverted wisdom if not an impossibly original darkness? When we begin in the absolute light of God, we expect ourselves, like the older brother in the prodigal's tale, to want to remain at home. But the issue for Augustine is not whether he can ever have a good answer to his questions, but whether not having an answer is itself a kind of clue, a plumb line into the mystery of his will. Perhaps he is being clued in to the essential truth of his individuality: that his will is his bottom line, that nothing in him runs deeper than that. I doubt whether his description in book 7 of his involuntary return to his mundane senses, sexual habit and all, can sustain this conclusion, but it is important to entertain, along with him, the possibility that it does. We can then begin to see how one of his most deeply held assumptions about his will—that it is most his when he sins—threatens to render the Word made flesh into the wrong kind of mystery.

### Debriefing on beauty

In the wake of his unsettling return to the world of his sexual habit, Augustine replays for himself, with selective focus, his experience elsewhere. He has just come down from a higher elevation of beauty. What should he be taking away from the trip? What needs to be emphasized, clarified, and preserved in his memory? The task before him is a debriefing of sorts: he reports to himself about where he has been, as if he has been, in some respects, a stranger to his own highest regard.

He begins his debriefing by reconstructing his ascent. This time he emphasizes the inner unfolding of his desire for beauty and not the divine hand that snatches him from his place of familiarity and puts him at creation's peak. At the familiar place, the bottom of his perspective, there is his usual appreciation for sensible beauties. He is nudged out of familiarity and up a step when he thinks to ask questions (*conf.* 7.17.23): "I asked about my approval of the beauty of bodies, celestial and terrestrial; I asked about what it was in me that was rendering summary judgment on changeable things and saying: this ought to be like this, that not like that." His line of inquiry puts him in touch with his own mutable mind. There he finds an interior energy (*vim interiorem*) with a dual aspect. Like any sentient creature, Augustine is able to take in a flood of sense impressions and organize them instantaneously into a world of (relatively) stable material objects. But this is an unreflective awareness. When his interior energy becomes self-reflective, Augustine adds the work of reason to sensibility. He starts to become aware of what he is bringing to his senses: not just the bare supposition of substance—the supposition of the thing that endures the change—but also the appraisal that renders the thing good or bad, appealing or repulsive.

In his debriefing, Augustine alludes to the two fundamental insights of self-awareness. One is that the mind cannot derive its standards for evaluating mutable things from mutable things. Those things shift in value, get better or worse, but the standard that the mind applies to them—think of it for now as a concept of value—cannot shift in the same way; if it did, then the mind would lose its capacity to conceive of change and chart the better course. Such a mind would still be a mind only in the degenerate way that a corpse is a body. The other insight of self-awareness follows upon the first, and it cuts more deeply into ordinary, largely unreflective consciousness. The self-aware mind comes to see that mind, being mutable, cannot self-generate a stable basis of judgment; the concepts that guide its evaluation of things change over time, sometimes for the better, sometimes not. (I have now a better notion of justice than I had when I was a child, but perhaps a diminished notion of joy.) Granted concepts generally change more slowly than do the things they conceptualize, but they do change. The adolescent Augustine does not have the same concept of erotic love as the older man who, having had to bury his adolescent son, wants to be (along with his church) the bride of Christ. One hopes for improvement of course, but the change is palpable all the same. When Augustine really takes to heart the mutability of even his concepts for speaking about change, his mind cracks open, struck as if by lightning, and he has his short-lived but direct opening to the unchangeable itself, or that which is (*id quod est*; *conf.* 7.17.23). He comes away from the encounter knowing in his depths that sameness is preferable to change; indeed the alternative preference is not readily conceivable. The changing things of this world speak only of God.

End of the debriefing. At one level, a fairly superficial one, it is clear what Augustine most wants to remember about his trip to unlikeness and the inassimilable God. He wants to remember who God is, and by remembering he means that he wants more than a moment's rapture. He wants a lifetime of stability with God, a home in a place of unlikeness. And what is keeping him from this? He tells us that he was too weak to translate vision into flesh and take his sustenance from God, the food so unlike his usual fare (*conf.* 7.17.23): "My ability to focus left me, and with my weakness resurgent I returned to familiar things, taking with me nothing but my memory for love—a desire scented, as it were, with the fragrance of what I was not yet able to consume." Having situated himself somewhere between a frustrated gourmand and a wistful lover, Augustine quickly revises the image and casts himself as an infant, too little to take in solid food. His hope is no longer for fixation in a spectacular vision but for divine care of his flesh, like a mother nursing her baby. It took him a while, well longer than it takes to change a metaphor, to bring himself to hope for this (*conf.* 7.18.24): "I had no hold of my God, the humble Jesus, not being humble myself, and I did not notice the lesson that his weakness was meant to teach."

Apparently this is what Platonists do not get about God. They do not get the gift of a divine show of weakness because they do perceive their need for it. They prefer their God to remain on top of a metaphysical mountain peak and wait for them there, while they work through their confusion of two worlds, one of flesh, the other of spirit. Augustine credits the apostle Paul, who had much to say in his letters about spirit and flesh, for having alerted him to this unchastened side of Platonism. "I began reading," writes Augustine (*conf.* 7.21.27), "and whatever truth I found in the Platonists I found there, along with a commendation of your grace—so that no one who sees should boast as if he were other than the recipient not only of the thing seen but also the power to see it." On this reading of Paul, Platonists come off as half-hearted boasters; they associate God with what they see, their own discipline of mind with the seeing. It is odd, as I have already suggested, for Augustine's Platonists to have seen what they have no means of seeing. But perhaps what Augustine means by having seen is less a flash of ecstatic insight than a lifetime's labor of compassion and self-knowledge. Granting that, there is still the very large question of what the connection is between the ecstatically revealed God, far removed from flesh, and Jesus of Nazareth.

## BEAUTY MEMORIALIZED

### From Plato to Paul

To get at the question ventured above, we are going to need a less superficial reading of Augustine's alleged discovery of that which is—the ground of being. In book 8 of *City of God*, a book preoccupied with the best and worst of pagan natural theology, the Platonists generally come off well. Above all Augustine praises them for having conceptualized better than anyone else the true nature of God. They do not make the terrible mistake of confusing God with something bodily, but more than that they have a precise sense of what makes God unique. Whereas all other beings are corruptible (unless God wills otherwise), God is the one being who is essentially at one with the good. This is the great Platonist insight, their sublime sense of God's absolute simplicity (*simplicitas*; *civ. Dei* 8.6): "It is not one thing that he exists, another that he lives, as if he were able to exist and not live; not one thing that he lives, another that he knows, as if he were able to live and not know; not one thing that he knows, another that he is well, as if he were able to know and not be well—no, to live, to discern, to be well, that to him is what it is to exist." When this notion of simplicity is mistakenly applied to finite, material being, it drives God into an existential cul-de-sac and then walls off the one way in, that of material contiguity; God will have become an untouchable material being, having in regard to everything else an entirely alien materiality. But because the Platonists know "that God is not a body" (*nullum corpus esse Deum*; *civ. Dei* 8.6), they are free to find in simplicity the source of everything else's coming to be.

For this they will need a heightened awareness. When Augustine attempts to describe the heightening, he begins with a basic distinction between two objects of perception. It will quickly become for him a distinction in perception. There is life (*vita*), and there is body (*corpus*). Life is superior to whatever body it happens to animate, and it requires a distinctive mode of perception—intelligible rather than sensible—to get at the profundity of the difference. Awareness of mere bodies, the *sensibilia*, is the lowest kind of awareness; when limited to *sensibilia*, the mind lacks a path to self-awareness. It cannot, thus limited, direct a life that rises above the conflict between blind appetite and aversion to pain. I will not venture to say whether a life that limited is really, for Augustine, a human possibility; it seems to follow from a degenerate perspective, not an original one. Whatever the case may be, a heightening of perspective always begins with a rudimentary love of beauty. Even the most simplistic delight in beautiful things—the *intellegibilia*—suggests to Augustine an open mind's eye (*civ. Dei* 8.6): "There is no corporeal beauty, not the fixity of a figure, not the rhythm of a sing-song, that is not the mind's to appreciate." Admittedly we do not have to be terribly self-aware to delight in nursery rhymes and simple shapes. The way forward requires the mind to catch itself in the act of loving beauty and notice the idea (*species*) that transcends the thing, the material bearer. Beautiful things prompt the mind's idea of beauty, but they do not own or originate the idea that they prompt. The idea comes from elsewhere, and its essential beauty can greatly, if not infinitely, dwarf its mutable prompt. Much depends on how materially fixated the mind of the viewer happens to be. The Platonists, whose minds, says Augustine, are the least distracted, see very clearly "that there is a place where the original idea (*prima species*) is beyond change and, for that reason, incomparable" (*civ. Dei* 8.6). But of course this place is less a place than a mode of being—uncreated but creative.

If we juxtapose Augustine's confessional debriefing with his analysis of the intelligibility of beauty in *City of God*, an ambiguity emerges. Is God the object of beauty in comparison to which the beauty of everything else is—to be as generous as possible—not much? Or does God supply us with the idea of beauty that endures through change? On the face of it, these are very different possibilities. If I seek the beauty that is God, then having it I have no conceivable beauty left to want—unless a lack of beauty is somehow beautiful. If Augustine is imagining himself at his peak loving God's beauty, then it is a very dark force indeed that drags him away and returns him to his love of beautiful things. But now consider God's idea of beauty. And keep in mind that Augustine's word for idea—corresponding to one of the Greek words for a Platonic form (εἶδος)—is *species*; it basically refers to whatever lends itself to looking, an appearance. If I were to have God's idea of beauty and that idea is, as Augustine suggests, my basis for seeing beauty in change, then I would see my changing world as God sees it, as an absolute beauty. This is the other beauty that Augustine may have seen at his peak, where he was pitched between God and the other things (*et cetera*). From there, creation struck him as perfect, but also as unfriendly to further revision. If he were to have added his unassimilated materiality—not yet idealized—to the picture, he would have been undoing perfection. The original idea of creation, being constitutionally changeless, rules out this possibility. Nothing material can be added to the idea, and materiality, apart from the idea, reduces to nothingness. Again Augustine credits the Platonists for their insight. They were able to see (*civ. Dei* 8.6) "that both body and mind were more or less endowed with idea (*speciosa*) and that if they managed to lack it altogether, they would not exist at all."

Perhaps our two possibilities—loving God, loving an idea of God—are not so different after all. God's beauty overpowers Augustine's perception and removes him from creation; God's idea of beauty perfects creation in Augustine's absence and keeps him from returning there. The doctrine of simplicity suggests that these are two sides of the same coin: God is not one thing, his idea of beauty another. But now we have a source of being that reduces all of us *ad absurdum*—not to derivative beings but to shadows of illusions. We cannot subsist and individuate in God, the all-absorbing beauty, and yet there is nowhere else, outside of God, for us to be. The only other option for existing, the material order of creation, is nothing if not God's idea of beauty. No truly mutable being is like that idea. Augustine's unlikeness—his place apart from both God and the created order—has become doubly perplexing: in itself and in relation to its antecedent condition. Before Augustine was unlike God or God's idea of beauty, what was he like? It is hard to see at this point how the simplified immaterial God is any easier for him to relate to than an idealized creation. In either case, he would be relating to beauty as privation relates to fullness. This is not a relationship; it is a corruption. And given God's immutability, it is not even a possible corruption.

But before we conclude that simplicity, the great Platonist insight into God, is a hopeless confusion, one that thoroughly undermines the distinction between creator and creature, we need to pay more attention to Augustine's assimilation of Plato to Paul. Everything that is worth taking from a Platonist is, Augustine insists, to be found in Paul, but in a better, more graceful form. Paul understands, as your average, puffed-up, spiritually self-important Platonist does not, that gratitude is of the essence of wisdom. Despite the character flaw of your average (and, yes, caricatured) Platonist, Augustine says that he is grateful for having loved Platonism before he ever learned how to read Paul and love Jesus; his disillusionment with Platonism, the best philosophy going, alerted him to the difference "between presumption and confession" (*inter praesumptionem et confessionem*; *conf.* 7.20.26).

Like many philosophically invested readers of Augustine, I have struggled to grasp the nature and import of the presumption that Augustine seeks to avoid. Does he mean that the Platonists presume too much on their own strength and so look futilely within themselves for the resources to break free of the dark and largely unconscious bodily forces that keep a soul bound to fear and blind appetite? If that is that case, does he think that God's incarnation in Christ is basically a gift of will, made available to those who give up their presumption and confess their weakness? If so, God will have entered into and embraced the flesh solely to break the claim that flesh has on life: Jesus is born of woman, lives and dies, but then has his death undone; his resurrection signals a new regime of spiritualized flesh, eternally secured from death by the will of his father. (And is not Paul the apostle of the resurrected Christ?) Augustine strongly suggests this line of interpretation when he speaks of Christ as the means by which Platonists find their way back to the fatherland, their happy-making place (*ad beatificam patriam*; *conf.* 7.20.26). Although they may sometimes have anticipatory moments of ultimate happiness, these tiny ecstasies come to them through grace and not by way of introspection, however well cultivated. It is only when they are moved to confess their utter dependence on God's flesh-conquering will that their moments add up and they begin, at least on one way of reading Augustine, to enter into life eternal.

Obviously I do not like very much this interpretation of Augustine's turn from Plato to Paul, even as I admit that Augustine himself suggests it. If what his God offers us over time is sufficient strength of will to break free from flesh and live a super-animated life, shielded from change, then the means to wisdom—a humble embrace of incarnation—becomes curiously extrinsic to wisdom's end, an eternity of immutable bliss. This is a picture that banks on the notion that knowing the good and being willing to live by it are entirely separate things. (God may be simple, but apparently we aren't.)

There is another, more compelling way to interpret Augustine's Pauline turn, and this way is equally his suggestion. After his topple from his peak experience and his fall back into fleshly habit, Augustine is made aware of his native weakness. His soul has no sticking power; it is too wed to its creature comforts to stay with God. Naturally Augustine hopes, with divine help, to grow stronger over time, but of course he will not avail himself of that help while he is still presuming upon his own strength. His presumption has a Platonist feel to it, although it is hardly just Platonist at root. On the strength of his breakthrough experience, brief but vividly memorable, Augustine styles himself a spiritual expert, a cognoscente of immateriality—infinity without extension, absolute simplicity, creative omnipotence, timelessness: "I chattered openly about all this," he recalls (*conf.* 7.20.26), "as if I were an expert, but until I began to seek the way to you in Christ, our redeemer, I was not skilled (*peritus*) but scuttled (*periturus*)." When Augustine does find his way of seeking years later, with his nose in Paul, he discovers his true strength (unimaginably) in the weakness of God. This is what happens to all those who cease, out of wisdom, to place faith in themselves (*conf.* 7.18.24): "At their feet they see divinity made weak from wearing the tunic of our skin; weary they prostrate themselves before it, but rising it lifts them up."

I take from this that Augustine's presumption has been as much about the nature of his weakness as about the source of his strength. If he misjudges or misses his presumption about his weakness, his admission of weakness is not going to help him seek the right kind of strength. False humility is just presumption by other means. So what then has he been assuming about his weakness and how it may differ from God's "tunic of skin"—the tunic of our mortality, albeit divinely retailored? And in what way (if any) have his assumptions been presumptuous? The topic, when pursued in depth, takes us into Augustine's complex doctrine of original sin, and I want to reserve the fuller discussion of that doctrine for the next chapter. For now I restrict my focus to a section in book 3 of *On Free Will*, a book that reflects his debt to Platonism but not his fervor for Paul. It dates from around the time of his ordination in 394, the main impetus for his plunge into Pauline exegesis. Toward the end of book 3, Augustine describes the natural condition of human weakness that is, more properly speaking, the penalty of sin (*lib. arb.* 3.19.54):

> What a person does wrongly out of ignorance; what he cannot do rightly, though he wants to—these are called sins and for this reason: they have their origin in the sin of a free will. That precedent of will warrants these sins, as its consequences. Consider: just as we apply the term tongue not only to the organ we move in our mouths when we speak but also to the consequence of that movement—the form and sound of the words that allow us to speak, say, of either the Latin or the Greek tongue, so we apply the term sin not only to sin in the strict sense, to that which is done knowingly and with a free will, but also to what has to follow from sin, as its punishment. So also we speak of nature with a double meaning: human nature, strictly speaking, refers to the original creation, a blameless kind of thing; it can also refer to the penalized condition into which we are born: mortal, ignorant, enslaved to flesh. In that sense, the apostle says (Eph. 2:3): "We also were naturally children of wrath, just like everyone else."

Augustine's Adam, the original sinner in the strict sense of sin, has, in stark contrast to his "children of wrath," an unburdened beginning: no angry divine father, just a loving creator; no great ignorance or difficulty, but wit enough to know better than to disobey God and taste death. For no good reason, Adam follows his partner, the woman, into disobedience, and the result, as described above, is procreation that is "naturally" mortgaged to God-alienated flesh. Augustine is aware that he has no explanation either for Adam's motive or for the mechanism by which Adam's heirs experience the effects of his sin—a clouded mind and a weakened will—as if his sin were theirs. His concern is not to account for the intimacy between natal human weakness and an unnatural desire to nurse on God's absence but to emphasize it. We are all born with untrustworthy natures, with needs that are bound to mislead us about what we *really* need. As hard as it is to explain this twisted kind of naturalness, Augustine insists that acceptance of its hold on us is the beginning of true responsibility; it is the first step of our return to the father's house.

If there is presumption in the weakness that Augustine attributes to all the children of wrath, himself included, it lies in the idea that human weakness has claim to a responsibility that is, as it were, more than divine. Think of the natal weakness of God, the infant life of Jesus. He has no inherited disposition to seek his life in God-alienated flesh. Do we imagine then that he has no inclination to nurse at his mother's breast? Augustine, of course, is not condemning human infants, God-alienated or not, for having human needs. Sin's penalty refers not to the fact of human need but to its dispiriting quality. If we live largely unconsciously, as unthinking servants to our appetites, we will tend not to notice that life in the flesh is always shared, most fundamentally with God. If we start to notice our not noticing, then it may seem as if we now know what God cannot possibly know: the terrible emptiness of sin, absolute aloneness. On the one hand, Augustine is disposed to turn that emptiness into a source of special human responsibility, individual and collective: it is all of us in Adam who turn from God and choose voluntarily to live in a wasteland. God cannot share in this responsibility of ours, not even as Jesus—especially not; such responsibility is the birthright solely of Adam's children, our badge of *moral* distinctiveness, grave though it be. On the other hand, Augustine experiences his emptiness as the place where he hears God call from afar. The history of his flesh soon returns to him, like an unfulfilled promise. Augustine will be tempted to ignore the promise and cling in his memory to his moment out of time. This is understandable. Really to share the same flesh with God, he would have to give up the special responsibility that has defined for him both his guilt and his moral identity. And how is that surrender not irresponsible?

Augustine does have a view, though never an entirely clear one, to a different kind of responsibility. This kind is more a matter of recognition than of willfulness, and it does not require him to trade in his innocence for his identity. It begins to insinuate itself, in shades of grey, in his labor of memory. Over time he works to remember the God of his creation-peak experience differently: no longer his life's great interruption, a moment of unbirthing, this God will prove to be the mother of his each and every moment. This is not just a change of remembered object; it is a change in the nature of memory itself. Simple recollection has now become a sacred act. Augustine mostly resists the sanctification of his memory, confesses to his lack of readiness. He would prefer, like most of us, to live in his own time, the time that fits to measure, or at least seems to, when he is not thinking much about it. The rest of time, alien and unbounded, washes over him like a solvent and removes him, bit by bit, from himself. Why sanctify that? He is honestly not sure why, but he begins to sense that profane time—the time for which *he* is the measure—is finally not memorable. I conclude with a few thoughts about the will-defying disquietude that frames his struggle to remember.

### The emotion of time

Francisco Petrarca (Petrarch) was both a great humanist of the Italian Renaissance and a lover of Augustine. While in the throes of a spiritual crisis, Petrarch took a pocket-sized copy of the *Confessions* with him to the top of Mount Ventoux in Southern France, opened the book at random, and put his trust in providence. He was not disappointed. The words he fell upon chastened his perspective on worldly achievement and changed his life (*conf.* 10.8.15):

> People travel to marvel at mountain peaks, great surging seas, broad river falls, the ocean's ambit, and the starry orb—and they leave themselves behind.

Petrarch ends there, but Augustine rounds off the thought:

> They don't marvel that when I was speaking of these things I was not seeing them with my eyes. And yet I would not be speaking of these things were I not seeing them in myself, as items of memory: the peaks, waves, rivers, and stars, all of which I have seen before, and the ocean, which I trust others to have seen. I was seeing them as big as life, as if they were on the outside.

It is tempting to hear in Augustine's sentiment, as Petrarch clearly did even in the truncated version, an invitation to turn within—like any good Platonist would—and discover there a world of great wonder, power, and beauty, a world far surpassing the sensible.

But in the sentences that preface the passage quoted above, Augustine is commenting on how impossible he finds it to keep track of all the images that enter his head. He forms images in his mind of whatever he sees or remembers having seen; he can even form an image of what he has never seen if he has some way of proceeding by analogy. He can, for instance, imagine the ocean; having seen a big sea—the Mediterranean—he begins with his image of that and then imagines something much bigger. He is not suggesting in this context that the image of a thing, being a mental expression, is more beautiful than the thing itself. In any case it does not follow from what he believes about beauty—that it takes a mind to perceive it—that the mind alone is beautiful. And certainly it would be implausible to the point of bizarre for him to be claiming that his mental image of the ocean is necessarily more awe-inspiring than the ocean itself. He has, after all, never even seen the ocean. What he finds truly amazing is the fact that his inner image-making factory is always out-doing itself (*conf.* 10.8.15): "Is the mind too narrow to encompass itself? Where is the part of it, then, that it does not grasp? Out of itself and not in? How does the mind not grasp itself? Many times I mull this over in my amazement, and I am left stupefied."

If Augustine were one of those people who seek to be captivated by material beauties, he might not have noticed or have been very impressed by the chaos of his inner life and its out-of-kilter imagery. When we see a thing, we do not for the most part take ourselves to be seeing an *image* of the thing; we see *the thing*, what's right before us. We take ourselves to be seeing an image of the thing only when we are struck by the partiality of our seeing. Say that I am looking at a rose of extraordinary beauty and delicacy; it is the jewel of my garden. For a captivated moment or two, I fail to consider that from another angle I may see the black spots that have been turning all my roses into withered shadows of themselves. I look from all sides and see, to my relief, that my beloved rose is spot-free. But I also realize, with the spell of its immediate beauty broken, that my seeing has been partial nonetheless. My rose does not exist only in the present moment. Like any material being, it has a past that I can potentially recollect and a future that I can more or less reasonably expect. At any given moment, what I see is what I see at present, but the image of something materially present always has a threefold aspect—a blending, but not always a harmonious one, of past, present, and future.

Augustine speaks, somewhat awkwardly, of a present of things past, a present of things present, and a present of things future: a conjunction in the mind of memory, seeing, and expectation (*conf.* 11.20.26). The unity of those three modes of apprehension depends on there being a present (*praesens*) that is common to past, present, and future; it is best thought of as a *presence*—that which is set before (*prae*) awareness (*sensus*). It is characteristic of material things that they are never entirely present in the present moment; partly they are constituted by what they have been (their presence in the past) and partly by what they will be (their presence in the future). It is a huge question for Augustine whether the mind's image of a thing ever rises to the level of complete awareness of what the thing is. There may be no single image that can deliver the requisite presence.

Now of course the mind is not just in the business of getting to know material things. There are items of knowledge that have no truck with images, none at all; they just show up in mental space, whole and as they essentially are, and the mind, itself imageless, immediately knows its like. Items in pure geometry and mathematics fall into this category. Consider the difference, says Augustine (*conf.* 10.12.19), between the lines in an architectural drawing, "thin as a spider's thread" but still seen with "the body's eye" (*carnis oculus*), and the lines that are perceived without the need of any kind of physical representation; we see them "on the inside" (*intus*). Similarly, Augustine continues, there is a big difference between a number of things and a number, which is not in any way material. I say the word, five, and count off five fingers; my young daughter, hoping to learn her numbers, nods approvingly and does likewise. If there is this big difference between a line in the mind and a line on a page, a number in the mind and a finger count, then I cannot hope to show her directly what an idea is. At best my physical gesticulations may prompt her to recall what only the "inner light of truth" (*interior lux veritatis*; *mag.* 12.40) can convey to her: the fullness of her inner world. For the person lacking in self-awareness and glued to material objects, Augustine has no argument, only pity (*conf.* 10.12.19): "Let him mock me as I speak of the mind's things, the one who does not see them; I feel for him mocking me."

It is tempting to Augustine to think of God as an immaterial entity, more sublime than a bit of mathematics, but grasped in essentially the same way: mind sees mind. In an early work, the *Soliloquies*, he imagines having a conversation with his own reason, *Ratio*, who is helping him into his knowledge of God and soul. He naively suggests to *Ratio* that God is not knowable to him in way that spheres, lines, and other ideal objects are. *Ratio* reassures him that he has overstated the difference (*sol.* 1.5.11): "It is a given that you will relish knowing God many times more than knowing these things, but the dissimilarity is a matter of different objects, not of modes of understanding" (*rerum tamen, non intellectus dissimilitudine*). This line of thinking finally stalls out for him as the mind begins to look, well, *too* immortal—eternally knowing and essentially untouched by a bodily history of birth, aging, and death. Book 3 of the *Soliloquies*, which was to be a proof that the mind is truly secure in its incorporeal and God-like point of view, never gets written. He has a brief go at this proof in *The Soul's Immorality* (*imm. an.*), a short study that he wrote to remind himself to finish the *Soliloquies*, but clearly he was not encouraged by the results (*retr.* 1.5.1): "Mainly because of its dense and abbreviated reasoning, this small book is obscure—so much so that it wears me out to read it, and I am scarcely able to understand myself."

In a later work, where God has reemerged with greater sublimity, Augustine is still banking on mind-to-mind correspondence, albeit now by way of analogy. Begin with the idea that the mind, when not unthinkingly confusing itself with material things, knows itself and its own nature immediately. "For what," asks Augustine rhetorically (*Trin.* 10.7.10), "is as present to cognition as the mind is, and what is as present to mind as the mind itself?" Self-presence still has for him a threefold aspect: the mind simultaneously recalls itself (past), sees itself (present), and wills itself to be continued (future). Now consider that even a triune mind with such perfect timing is but an image (*imago*, but literally imageless) of true perfection. Here is Augustine again (*Trin.* 15.22.43): "The Trinity as it is in itself—that is one thing; the image of the Trinity in something else—that is another." By the time he ends his great work on the Trinity, it will have become clear to him that his self-comprehension is necessarily too puny to house Father, Son, and Spirit; the image can never contain the source. And yet it is on the supposition that his mind can contain *itself* and exist as a limited whole that he is able to model a perfection greater than his own, an infinite whole. His idea of God comes through and then transcends his idea of self.

In the *Confessions*, Augustine is amazed to discover that he does not have a coherent idea of self, nothing that he can wrap his mind around. At any given moment, he is witness to a sliver of himself, but that sliver is constantly being reshaped and eroded by the great flow of images that race through his present and pool into his past, where they dwell in memory. When he speaks in awe of "the great force of memory" (*magna vis memoriae*; *conf*.10.10.15), "too great" he adds (*magna nimis*; *conf.* 10.10.15), he is not referring to his ability, not very great at all, to retrieve images from his memory and convert them into a self-conception; he is referring to his memory's silent witness against all his solo efforts at self-conceiving. Either there is always too much for him to recollect, too much experience to sort out, or there is something deep in his memory, some "great force," that actively resists his drive for self-containment.

When he confesses, near the beginning of his meditation on memory, to having traveled away from God and toward himself—a prodigal's walk in the dark—his words are especially striking given his sometime tendency to make a virtue of self-presence (*conf.* 10.5.7):

> Without a doubt we now look through a glass darkly and not yet face to face, and because of this, for as long as I travel away from you, I am more present to me than to you. But I do know this about you, that you can in no way be undone. As for me, I do not know which trails I can weather and which I cannot. I have hope because you can be trusted: you do not let us be tried beyond our ability to bear, but build an exit into the trial, so that we can endure. Let me then confess to you what I know of me; let me also confess what I do not know. For what I know of me I know when you dawn on me, and what I do not know of me I do not know until such time as my darkness is made high noon before your gaze.

There is no suggestion here that Augustine is most a knower when his mind is self-relating and he has access to an immediate, if limited, form of knowing. On the contrary, he is looking for some distance to open between his self-certainties and his life's potential, a crack for different light to come in. Darkness too. He seems, for now, to be open to the coincidence of opposites, light and dark, spirit and flesh. His inner darkness—usually for him his dark love of flesh—may be, for all he knows, high noon for God. What does he really know of what God can illuminate? What does he know of himself? The great force of memory is there to remind him that he is, as a creature of time, perpetually behind and ahead of himself: some of him is no longer, some not yet. If he resolves in response to identify with a mind that is distracted but never undone by the unfolding of material things, then he will surely lose his awe for the force that deposits him in time. Why care if he is not really there? Otherwise he gets all the distance between him and himself that he could ever want. The question is: what does he want?

Augustine assumes that time must be a good thing, being God's creation, but he finds time hard to love. It breaks up into a future that is not yet, a past that is no longer, and a present that gets whittled down to a pivot between two forms of non-being. Time's one sliver of being, the present time, is made to pass away; if the present never passed, time would not be time—it would be eternity. It just does not seem possible to Augustine to love something that exists only because "it tends not to" (*conf.* 11.15.17). The mind that distends itself to embrace a time-defined beloved tends also not to exist. So why isn't the love of temporal things merely self-defeating? Augustine admits that he has no sense of time beyond what his mind has managed to embrace and contain. He seems determined, in fact, to measure time in terms of his mind's affection for time (*conf.* 11.27.36): "Either time is the affection, or I do not measure time." The irony of his ultimatum lies in the fact that his mind cannot contain time. Time to the mind is an emotion, and Augustine's term for a mental affection, *affectio animi*, can signal an emotion—a move outwards. If Augustine contains time in his mind, then his mind no longer contains itself. Once again he is returned to the great force of memory.

It turns out that Augustine can no more resolve to love things in time than he can resolve to exempt his mind from time and live in eternity. The only issue to be resolved is whether God can love temporal beings and not be undone. And that is up to God to resolve. Augustine can only report on the effect that a divine resolution has had on his affection (*conf.* 10.27.38):

> Late I loved you, beauty so old and so new; I loved you late. And look, you were within and I was without; and there I was seeking you, where I shipwrecked my misshapen self on the beauties of your making. You were with me and I was not with you; the beauties which exist only if they exist in you kept me at a distance. You called and shouted and finally shattered my deafness; you

were radiant, resplendent—my blindness you put to flight. You were perfumed; I inhaled and gasp for you. I have taken my taste, and now I feel hunger and thirst. You touched me, and I burn for your peace.

Augustine gets returned to his senses. But it is easy to be misled here, if we draw the wrong moral from his suggestion that God was within him while he was on the outside, indulging his prodigal love of misconstrued beauty. The bare implication, of course, is that Augustine needs to be within himself to be with his source. True, he cannot live forever in a wasteland of his own making, where he insists on reducing his every act of love to an exercise in self-privation. He needs to embrace his more substantial self and find God there, once again dividing Augustine from himself—but this time without alienation. Unlikeness will have become natural and full of promise. What we need to grasp, in order to grasp this, is that Augustine's awakened desire is for a beginning as well as a consummation. He gestures to a shared life in the flesh, with God on the outside and Augustine within. He gestures to a life lived in anticipation of a birth.

## CHAPTER THREE

## SEX AND THE INFANCY OF DESIRE

*The poet was a fool who wanted no conflict among us, gods or people. Harmony needs low and high, as progeny needs man and woman.*
                                            Heraclitus (trans. Haxton)

Imagine that the self you call your own is really a union of two selves—one higher, one lower—and that the relationship between them is dodgy. Your higher self is looking to perfect its union with something that is eternally perfect and perfectly good; it will think of that more perfect union as its redemptive knowledge. Your lower self is not terribly clear about what it wants, not being given to profound self-reflection, but from the higher perspective, it looks to be trying to perfect its union with its body, the thing it thinks of, quite precipitously, as its essential form. You may be tempted, at this point in the imaging, to style yourself as an onlooker, neither the one self nor the other, but some third thing between. Consider the possibility that there is no between here. Either you feel yourself being drawn up, against the weight of habit, into an elevated desire, or you feel yourself being weighted down, despite your noblest intent, by needy flesh. You may feel yourself at times to be both selves at once, but there is no issue from this coincidence other than heightened inner conflict. When death comes, as it must, and soul is sundered from body, soul either goes the way of decomposing flesh, as the lower self always feared it would, or soul becomes liberated from flesh and the higher self survives. Or perhaps I should say, more tentatively, that some self—maybe higher, maybe not—survives death and decomposition.

 Bear with me as I invite you to replay the imagining in an altered key. You are the postmortem self, soul without body. Do you have any reason to want your body back and with it the life that left you divided between a higher and lower self? This way of putting the question assumes, of course, that your postmortem self is your higher self. If it were your lower, you would be wanting your body back because you persist in wanting to perfect yourself in bodily terms—you see no alternative. Meanwhile your higher self, having also survived your body's demise, is still struggling to break from you or, more precisely, from your obsession with composed (and therefore decomposable) unities. Basically this is the same imagining as before. The postmortem framing is irrelevant. The new possibility I want you to consider is that your higher self conjoins with your lower, body-oriented self out of higher purpose and desire and not because of some unaccountable force that holds opposites together. But I should not be asking you to be imagining a postmortem, disembodied life. Imaging the life that you have now is challenging enough. So return to those two selves of yours, still in a dodgy relationship, but now defined as much by mutual attraction as by repulsion.

Your higher self loves your lower self. And out of love it wants to teach that self a better way, much as a parent, with reserves of patience, commits to educating its slow-to-learn child. It takes little imagination to live within the limits of a narrow self-love. We commonly think of such a life as selfish—as if it were peculiarly revelatory of self. In fact there is no non-circular way to identify the self in selfishness. You say that you are your body and your body alone, that you feel only its pains and pleasures. How do you know which body is yours? Well, it is the body whose pains and pleasures you most directly feel. We are sufficiently familiar with our lower selves not to be especially bothered by the circularity of such reasoning. We should be careful about becoming overly familiar. Do you really want to claim that you never feel what others feel? That all you ever sense is, in effect, one body, variously stimulated? Certainly you can commit to this way of thinking and remain consistent with the self you have imagined your body to be, but now you risk not noticing how little you have imagined. Perhaps you would do better to admit how your capacity to love can sometimes make it hard for you to know which body claims you most. This is a difficulty that your selfish lower self can scarcely appreciate apart from a higher inspiration.

So far I have given you only a condescending higher self to imagine. This self stoops down from a sublime height and tries to instill its constant desire—for eternal things—into the consciousness of its lower counterpart. The inspiration begins to take effect when the lower self no longer feels the need to translate all love into self-love. To get a sense of what I mean by this, think of the two fundamentally different ways in which the neighbor-love command—the command to love your neighbor as yourself—can be rendered. In one you begin with your own self-love, bring it into focus, and then extend it to a self-image, your neighbor, now your satellite self. In the other the neighbor is simply and directly the self to be loved. There is no transfer or extension of a (supposedly) more basic self-love. If you are a lower self who can manage neighbor-love along the lines of the second rendering, then your condescending higher self is moderately pleased. You know that you have it within you not to confuse your self with your body; now you just need to learn how not to confuse it with the body of someone else. Your higher self will want to return you to your self-love, but at a greater depth—where you start to realize that you are no more your body than you are your neighbor's body.

I am not going to go into this further lesson of the higher self (which I confess I have never learned); instead I am going to give you a higher self that descends rather than condescends and weds its love to flesh. Its story goes something like this. Your higher self loves you, not because it loves itself in you (neighbor-love, first rendering), but because you are the self that it loves (neighbor-love, second rendering). Whenever you realize that love is not always transferred self-love, the lower part of you ascends and the higher part descends. This contrary motion makes for an uneasy incarnation. Your lower self, in ascending, is loving bodies other than its own, and your higher self, in descending, is materializing the self that it loves. In place of a presumptive unity of self with self, we get distention: the stretch of a self wanting both to self-surrender and to take root. And it is no longer clear, if it ever really was, which impulse is higher and which not.

Plotinus, who, along with Paul, does most to shape Augustine's sense of the ambiguities of spirit, has been the background inspiration for my opening imaginary. In his tractate on soul's descent into body (*enn.* 4.8)—an early treatise and likely well known to Augustine—Plotinus reflects on his many ecstatic experiences, when his soul has left his body and reached to its ultimate source, and wonders why, each and every time, he ends up back in his body. There seems to be no reason for his soul to prefer beautiful bodies, which are all shadowy things, barely able to hold a form, to the abundance of the One, which floods the mind with beauty and fixes soul in intellect. The word soul (Ψυχή) needs to be used advisedly here. Plotinus lets us refer, in a rough and ready way, to individual souls that animate bodies. In this manner, I can talk about my soul, you yours. But if this is the only way we can think to talk about soul, then we will have forgotten ourselves and are bound for sorrow. Soul is more fundamentally All-Soul (ὅλη Ψυχή), a unified form of divine intellect and the administrator of all animation in the sensed world. As reflections of All-Soul, individually ensouled beings are disposed both to crave higher knowledge (an ecstatic endeavor) and to care for material things (a mundane undertaking). In the All-Soul, knowledge and nurture are perfectly wed; in individual souls the caring impulse mysteriously outpaces the knowing impulse, to the benefit of neither. I will end up, while oblivious of my higher nature, serving an ever narrowing vision of myself—from globe, to country, to family, to body, to body-image. My footloose soul will have unaccountably traded the bliss of divine communion for a self-defeating life of separateness.

The account that Plotinus offers of why soul descends into body (and I am thinking primarily of *enn.* 4.8.4) is less explanatory than it seems. Suppose that I try to use it as an explanation for my life's confusions. Basically I am being told that I get into trouble when I think I know better than my higher self how to run my life. I am wrong when I think this way, of course, and my adolescent soul inevitably succumbs to its own arrogance (τόλμα) and starts to look pathetically needy. My arrogance doubtless explains my fall, but what explains my arrogance? If my soul proceeds from the All-Soul, then I have never not known the boon of life in my father's house (i.e., life in the Divine Intellect, Νοῦς, to which the maternal All-Soul eternally clings). I have no motive to go prodigal.

But this way of putting the problem is misleading. I do not exist as a lower self, struggling to regain its higher perspective, until I have left my father's house, divided my soul against itself, and suffered privation. If there were a good explanation for why I do this, I would not be able to understand it, not while I lived divided. Only from my original oneness could I understand, but from there, presumably, I would have no need of an explanation. My existence in both spirit and flesh would feel like oneness.

When Plotinus wonders why his soul returns to his body, having regained its oneness, he is not preparing us to think that he is the sort of teacher who obsessively refuses the fruits of his own spiritual labor. If his soul descends, that can only be because there is no necessary fracture of soul in such descent. But those of us who confuse incarnation with spirit's conflict with flesh still have work to do. The short story that Plotinus tells us about obsessiveness, disguised as soul, discloses in general terms the nature of the work. To take our place in things, we must learn how to ascend and leave our fictions of soul and body behind us.

While there are certainly echoes of Plotinus in Augustine (who is likewise apt to question, without condemning, soul's love of body), Augustine tends to invert the Plotinian itinerary. Plotinus ascends in order to descend and bring light into a cave of ignorance, where many live unlike themselves. Augustine tells his soul (*conf.* 4.12.19), "Descend, so that you may ascend, and ascend to God." Take ascent and descent in this context to refer to orientations of attention. If you are ascending, you are paying less and less attention to how you have loved the body, and your first step up is not away from your attraction to physical beauty (here it is always possible for one body to stand in for another) but from your love of somebody in particular. The presumption of ascent is that you cannot think of love as your desire to preserve or perfect a body and truly understand what it is that makes you love. You need distance from your desire. The path of descent, from some peak of abstracted awareness all the way down into the depths of a particularized love, is no simple reversal of ascent. Think of the climatic moment of Augustine's interiorized ascent from carnal affection to love of God (*conf.* 7.17.23): at the very moment he makes the heady discovery that he is already the lover he wants to be (*iam te amabam*), his old habit of desiring flesh grabs him by the soul and drags him back down to a shadowy place—part matter, part illusion. His journey can be considered a descent and not a fall from grace when he is able to take his best love with him into the shadows and find all of his family there, his humanity root and branch; then his love of flesh will be entirely voluntary, a gift of spirit.

When I say that Augustine is, spiritually speaking, more of a descender than a climber, I do not mean to suggest that he has a cheerier attitude toward the body and its needs than does Plotinus.

Both men believe that a spiritual aspiration styled as a bodily appetite is bad news. If they are right, you cannot trust your desire for God nor I my hankering after the One if we are both simply redirecting a lower form of desire—as in scratching an itch, releasing a tension, quieting a hunger, or even vying for glory—toward an allegedly more sublime object. It is more the form of our desire that has to change. On that score Augustine and Plotinus supply us with different models of success. Plotinus gives us no reason to doubt his ascending. Many times he has left his body to be with the One; many times he has returned—until all the little deaths finally give way to the big one. With Augustine matters are less clear. Is the ascent he describes in book 7 of the *Confessions* an honest, all-the-way-to-God ascent, the peak of wisdom?

Considering that his flesh-bound habit is still able to reach him at his highest, most liberated height, I suspect not. Plotinus is puzzled, much as any theorist would be, by his soul's desire for his body; he inquires about it from a place of equanimity within himself. Augustine seems to have no such place. His post-ascent feelings of self-division, which reach a fever-pitch in book 8, suggest that he wears his carnal desires close to his heart. They do not fade away or conform to spirit over the course of a contemplative ascesis; instead they bide their time and wait, like so many hungry stowaways, to plead exigency. His soul's ascent partially illuminates for him his soul's native love of God; mostly it shows him the unfinished business of his incarnation. As this business, he learns from Paul, is fundamentally God's business, Augustine cannot fairly claim to have been with God and not with himself, flesh and all. In that regard, the real success of his ascent lies in its check on his presumption.

Augustine's turn to Paul, which he details for us near the end of book 7, is less his rejection of Plotinus than his recognition that Paul, for him a Platonist *manqué*, is in the better position to be his guide to God's descent—the divine way into the flesh. This may be because, to follow his suggestion in book 7, that Paul shows more humility in his person than a self-described Platonist does, or, more to the point, that his texts do. Augustine fails to find in Platonist literature (e.g., the *Enneads*) any comparable mention of a troubled spirit, a contrite heart, tears of confession, a people's salvation, Christ's sacrifice, or the pouring forth of his Holy Spirit, "the cup of our salvation" (*poculum pretii nostri; conf.* 7.21.27). But however the contest of humility works out (I am loathe to entertain it), I think that there is a deeper, less *ad hominem*, reason for Augustine's Pauline sensibilities. Paul allows Augustine to play out Plotinian ambiguities of spirit—flesh fleeing, flesh affirming—as a drama of two Adams, two paradigms of the human. The first Adam, apparently motherless, values his tie to his partner, the woman, over his obedience to his father in heaven; the second Adam, born of woman but begotten of that same father, remains obedient and redeems for the first Adam's descendents the promise of deathless flesh. For someone whose ties to women remain achingly close to his aspirations for spiritual transcendence, Paul's invitation to spiritualize mortal flesh will seem nearly irresistible. But it is also true that the disparity between mother-born flesh, bound to die, and father-restored flesh, preserved for heaven, tugs at the seams of Augustine's theology and threatens to undo its coherence.

Being too inventive a theologian to borrow, Augustine is finally no more Plotinian in his use of Plotinus than he is Pauline in his use of Paul, and his amalgam of those two (really disparate) inspirations is the further expression of his own genius. That genius takes him, among other places, to his notorious doctrine of original sin, praised by some as a *sine qua non* of the Christian faith, condemned by others as a thinly veiled piece of misogyny. No one disputes the centrality of the doctrine to Augustine's theology. My own view is that the doctrine suffers from its association with an overly simplified mythology. The simplification is not Augustine's. I look to his more complex story and some of its implications—especially for his sense of his own conversion—in what follows.

## THE MYTHOLOGY OF SIN

### Grace and original guilt

Augustine's doctrine of original sin takes in two, intimately related concerns with origin: there is the question of what first moves human beings, made to love God, to fragment that love and live partial, death-haunted lives; and then there is the further question—call it the genetic question—of how a choice becomes an inheritance. In Augustine's parsing of these questions of origination, Adam and Eve, our ancestral parents, have no inherited disposition to sin but choose to sin anyway (a mystery of psychology), and we, who are their descendents, enter life disposed to sin and choose a better life only when divinely aided to do so (a mystery both of grace and genetics). Augustine never would have had a distinctively genetic question to face had he been willing to allegorize his Adam and Eve, leaving them to represent universal aspects of soul. Then he would have had only a single mystery to fathom: the soul's choice, against its better wisdom, of an imperfect love. His first commentary on Genesis, directed against the crude literalisms of the Manichees, is in fact mostly allegorical, and there he tries out the notion of an originally incorporeal Adam and Eve (*Gn. adv. Man.* 1.19.30). But the notion never sits well with him.

Human beings, he comes to believe, have from the beginning been composites of spirit and flesh; they are not souls masquerading in bodies or yoked to the body as if to some dispensable and altogether temporary contrivance. Adam and Eve are to Augustine flesh and blood originals; they have to have sex in order to reproduce, and their garden life in Eden, however brief and dream-like (it was before they had children), is a part of human history. We can no longer retrieve that part. The place where it took place is inaccessible to us, being under angelic guard (Gen. 3:24), and even if we could get to it, we would be fundamentally unlike the people who once lived there. Adam and Eve were given the wisdom to know how and why not to sin; we have inherited, by contrast, a beginning in "ignorance and mortal toil" (*lib. arb.* 3.20.55). It would not be equitable, Augustine contends, for the first couple, once having sinned, then to be able to produce enlightened children, endowed with forfeited wisdom. Our hobbled start in life is thus part of sin's dread penalty (*lib. arb.* 3.19.54), and although Augustine is not wholly clear about this point, it seems primarily a penalty visited upon our original parents that we, their children, can never naturally surpass them. When he imagines us complaining that our lot is too hard and grossly unfair, he concedes that we would have a point were it not true that we have recourse to divine aid and need only ask to receive its benefit (*lib. arb.* 3.19.53): "You are not at fault because you don't hold your wounded parts together, but because you disregard the one willing to heal them."

Augustine in any case does not rush to the view that we rightly bear the guilt of someone else's past, even if that someone is a close relative. He knows the difference between a sexually transmitted disease and a corrupted household. The first is an affair of the flesh, at least in so far as the mechanism of transmission is at issue. I may will to have sex, but my newborn does not will (cannot in fact will) to catch the disease that carries through my act. The second is a matter of soul. I may model sin to my growing child, but my sin transfers only to the degree that my child freely consents to it—a tricky judgment, but we know what to look for: the emergence in the child of free will, *liberum arbitrium*. The regulating intuition in both cases is that spirit, not flesh, is the realm of freedom, and thus spirit, unlike flesh, is subject only to self-willed corruption. It proves to be a devilishly hard intuition for an embodied spirit, like a human being, to sustain with any consistency, but Augustine never rejects it outright. It comes then as a rather discordant moment in his theology when he first feels compelled to speak of guilt (*originali reatu*; *Simpl.* 1.2.20) as an involuntarily human inheritance, making the whole race into a birthed lump of sin-infected flesh (*massa peccati*; *Simpl.* 1.2.16). Now we can start worrying about which part of hell houses unbaptized infants—Augustine thinks "the mildest" (*mitissima*; *pecc. mer.* 1.16.21).

What changes most fundamentally for him is his sense of divine parenting. It thickens as he struggles to interpret Paul's claims about election—especially the sheer gratuity of it—in Romans 9 (*Simpl.* 1.2). Augustine starts to think that God doesn't wait for Jacob or for any favored son and daughter to find the internal wherewithal to come to a sober self-assessment and petition for help. It is not the petition that occasions the parenting but the parenting that stirs in a person, sooner or later, the virtue of faith—trust that the God of life is still out there and even within. The logic of such parenting defies the reassuring division of labor between the soul that makes choices and the body that has impulses. In this life we are never fully responsible beings, passing judgment on our childish impulses from a place of sublime maturity; we enter the kingdom of heaven as children, still under the watch and nurture of God. When Augustine considers how good people fall and better people emerge from a place of fallenness (he has in mind Paul's history as a persecutor), he comes to what he believes is the only possible conclusion: that God elects wills (*voluntates eligantur*; *Simpl.* 1.2.22)—whole persons and not just their piecemeal psychologies. "But the will itself," he adds, "is not able to be moved in the slightest unless something happens to delight and stir the mind."

It is worth pausing to consider what he means by this. Is grace a providentially designed offering of beauty that triggers a person's latent disposition to become good, even saintly? We can imagine that Saul the persecutor is deep down the Paul that loves Jesus and fights the good fight. We can further imagine that Paul takes over from Saul—deep self replacing surface persona—only when Saul is suddenly blinded by a light from heaven and one of his former enemies lays hands upon him, helpless, and removes the scales from his eyes (Acts 9:1–19). The mind is stirred; the heart is delighted. The problem with this picture is that it leaves the deep self largely out of the work of grace. This is a self to be unearthed but not created *ex nihilo*; it enters the picture already in place, albeit buried at first. This won't do. Augustine no longer thinks of election as being based on a prior good, even a good as modest as an unexpressed disposition for some virtue; he explicitly rejects faith-based elections. Anyone who misses this point in his responses to Simplician need only wade a little into his anti-Pelagian writings to get the message. But the converse picture, suggested by his late-in-life reflections on predestination and perseverance (*persev.*; *praed. sanct.*; both written *c*. 428), is not so helpful either. Suppose that God creates absolutely *everything* about Paul's saintliness: his saintly predisposition (hidden at first), his altered self-awareness, his persistence in his saintly life. Where did Saul come from? To answer that kind of question, Augustine thickens our Adamic parentage, nearly to the degree that he has thickened grace. We end up with competing paternities: one father, partnerless, creates autonomously; the other father prefers to create with his partner, flesh of his flesh, even at the cost of his spirit (cf. Gen. 3:6: "she gave to her man, and he ate."). The resolution of this conflict is the work of grace—not the creation of unmixed goodness out of an unresisting void, but the miraculous emergence of something distinctively human out of a disposition, still of radically uncertain origin, to resist divine life.

We are back to the one great mystery of sin's motive. What moves Adam, or better, what moves us, to turn love of flesh into a prison-house of spirit? The genetic mystery of inherited guilt becomes a false issue for Augustine once he relocates the wayward Adam to the graced soul and reduces him there to a lingering resistance—internal to the psyche but not inherited. Now we get saints with troubled histories and an allegorical Adam. Augustine's attempt to hold onto a literal Adam, a man of ancient history, fails here. Adam loses his letter the moment he becomes a perverse spirit. From then on he has only an accidental connection to the body that would have been, from a literal point of view, his own. His sin—and I use the possessive pronoun very loosely—is no more intimately tied to one body than another. The same logic holds for the rest of us sinners.

Solidarity in sin is not a context for differentiating flesh. Augustine is right to speak of humanity as an undifferentiated mass (*massa*) and not as a collection of individuals whenever sin is being made out to be a procreative principle. But he is wrong, and wrong by virtue of his own best insights, when he invokes inherited guilt to define an alternative, albeit damned, genealogy of the human—as this is to attribute to sin precisely the procreative, life-extending power that it lacks.

### Adam, Eve, and the angels

Let's take a closer look at Adam's sin. I refer to Adam as decoupled from Eve and not to their collective enterprise of sin because it is Adam alone, claims Augustine, who is of a mind to sin. His Eve, the sensualist of the couple, feels her way unthinkingly into sin's deception. When the cunning serpent suggests to her that knowledge is life, she begins to see the tree in the middle of the garden differently. Augustine presumes that she is looking at the forbidden tree of knowledge (Gen. 2:17), but the Genesis text is vague about this, perhaps deliberately. The tree, life or knowledge, has become for her "a lust to the eyes" and so "she took of its fruit and ate" (Gen. 3:6). Lust is not very thoughtful. Augustine's Adam thinks about the stakes when Eve offers him a bite from her piece of fruit, and for various unstated reasons—which Augustine will venture to state—he decides to bite.

Augustine cites Paul as his authority for emphasizing gender roles in the drama of the first sin: Adam plays the soberly self-aware part; Eve gets to be seduced. "Adam was not led astray," Augustine writes, paraphrasing Paul (1 Tim. 2:14; *civ. Dei* 14.11), "but his woman was." While there is no way to remove the taint of sexism from a differentiation that tends to leave men with minds and women with bodies, Augustine is not entirely crude about its application. He proceeds on the assumption that male and female denote inalienable aspects of every single human being. But every single human being is also, from a more strictly corporeal point of view, either male or female.

One place where the complexity of his ambidextrous soul is conspicuously on display is book 12 of *The Trinity*, where Augustine's main business is to discredit the notion that a family triangle—father, mother, and son—provides an apt image of God's triune way of being. When God declares in Genesis 1:26, "Let us make a human in our image," Augustine takes the use of the first-person plural to indicate a Trinitarian imperative: this is God speaking to God as Father, Son, and Spirit. It follows for him that the human image of God has to be triune—three elements, perfectly coordinated. The next verse is going to test his assumptions about the *imago Dei* (Gen. 1:27): "And God created the human in his image, in the image of God He created him, male and female He created them." To keep this verse from implying that God's image is duplex, male and female, Augustine has to insert a full stop where I have put, following Robert Alter's translation, the second comma. God creates humankind in the divine image. Period. With the image fully in place, God's next move is to create sexual difference.

If this is the right way to punctuate the verse—and Augustine seems to think that it is (*Trin.* 12.6.6)—then sexual difference is excluded from the human image of God: it is either extrinsic to it, like a veil of clothing, or a distortion, like some disease. But Augustine is not anxious to claim either of those possibilities, for he still thinks of sexual difference as an originally human good and so part of even our idealized humanity. The problem he has given himself, when it comes to squaring image and reality, is basically this: he does not want God to have to stoop to a body-image, much less a gendered one, but nor does he want, in his ascendant self-image, to have to hate the flesh.

His solution—if we want to call it that—is to look for a suitably etherealized way to admit a "feminine" concern for the body into his Trinitarian economy. He lands on the expedient of casting knowledge of earthly things (*scientia*) as female and knowledge of eternal things (*sapientia*, often translated as wisdom) as male. Our minds are male, so to speak, when we are directly contemplating God, the one essentially eternal being; they are female when we cling to God's ideas (*aeternis rationibus*; *Trin.* 12.7.12) and use them to stabilize our otherwise chaotic perceptions of things in time. These are not equally lofty forms of knowing in Augustine's eyes. Only one in fact makes it into the image of God; the other, while dependent on contemplation for its ideas, is oriented less to God than to care and concern for the body (though not necessarily one's own). Augustine invokes a hard saying from Paul to symbolize the difference between the two forms of knowing (1 Cor. 11:7; *Trin.* 12.7.9): "Man ought not cover his head, for he is the image and glory of God. But woman is the glory of man." Since he is confident that Paul is not fool enough to be saying that flesh-and-blood women look less like an incorporeal God than flesh-and-blood men do, he is happy here not to be so literal-minded: the saying really means, he surmises, that we are closer to God when our minds are freed from bodily cares. But why imagine that woman is an apt symbol for a mind more laden? Augustine leaves it at this (*Trin.* 12.7.12): "It is because she differs sexually (*sexu corporis*) from man that woman could suitably symbolize through her body's veil (*in eius corporali velamento*) the part of reason that gets diverted to time-management."

I take it that two things are being veiled in Augustine's figuration (via Paul) of woman. One is the purely contemplative orientation of the mind, of which men and women, he thinks, are both equally capable; the other is what makes a woman physically a woman—not her head, but her sexuality, which affords her, for a time, the capacity to double life (or more than double it) from within. She is most naturally a time-manager—or really a time-giver—when she is bearing and raising her children.

If we keep in mind the literal basis of Augustine's figuration, we will be less likely to think of rerouted contemplation, from God to flesh, as an exercise in selfishness. I suppose that a mother's love for her child can be selfish if it amounts to no more than transferred self-love, but it is perverse to insist on that possibility. Sometimes a mother just loves her child, and, of course, it is not only mothers who are capable of love. They are just the ones who most obviously suggest the beloved's origination in the body. If Augustine means to cut out the care of temporary things, like children, from his image of God, then he risks turning the body-contempt of pure contemplation into a form of selfishness. My body, after all, is not just for me to use; it is sometimes quite naturally put to the service of others, whom I call, non-possessively, my own. But Augustine does not mean to *exclude* care of the body from the divine image; he means to *subordinate* the knowledge that goes into this care to a contemplative ideal. Here is where matters get even more complicated—and perhaps confused.

Consider the perfectly ordered mind: the sublimely male part, though mainly in love with eternity, condescends to his preoccupied but still obedient partner and lends her access to eternal ideas.

She ascends part of the way to him, in that her obedience to him renders her contemplative; he descends part of the way to her, in that his care for her renders him practical. If we could imagine their perfect place of meeting, where difference is without alienation and where duality is too generous not to be three, we may yet get to the human image of the triune God that Augustine, throughout the second half of *The Trinity*, so tirelessly seeks. But he would not expect us to be able to do that and still be thinking in terms of sexual difference. By the end of book 12, he has definitely come to think of the trinity of man, woman, and child as the image of a lower form of consciousness, too caught up with the things of the outer man (*hominis exterioris*; *Trin.* 12.15.25) to count as sublimely human. Augustine has a hard time imagining how the perfectly ordered mind can busy itself with mortal things without first having to compromise (and so in some sense reject) its enjoyment of God. Or to rephrase his difficulty in the language of Genesis: why does Adam even want a partner? Shouldn't life with God be enough? And yet it is God himself who says (Gen. 2:18): "It is not good for the human to be alone."

It is a striking feature of Augustine's reading of the Genesis myth that his Eve is much the same before and after her transgression. True, she is definitively mortal only afterwards, but her peculiar form of sentience, though not easy to describe, remains constant. Augustine politely rejects the notion, coming to him from respected defenders of the Catholic faith, that Eve embodies animation that is as much animal as human (*Trin.* 12.13.20, but cf. *Gn. adv. Man.* 2.11.15). He prefers to keep his Eve distinctively human. She seems to represent for him a reasoning person's desire for immortality, for fuller life, but before reason has put a final form to that desire. If a form-bestowing mind can be conceived to have an original tie to a formless depth, then Eve, who, for Augustine, is more moved than mover, is the pathos of that depth. Her one initiative is to offer her partner, the man, a share in her experience.

When Augustine considers Adam's motives for wanting to preserve his connection to the woman, he presents us with a man moved by pride and pity to save the partner who is, quite literally, a part of him (Gen. 2:22). She needs saving, Adam assumes, because she is, as the sole transgressor, too much on her own, and "she would wither away without his care" (*Gn. litt.* 11.42.59). He takes pity on her and condescends to join her in transgression, knowing full well that he is, by disobeying, inviting death into his life (Gen. 2:17): "From the tree of knowledge, good and evil, you shall not eat, for on the day you eat from it," God warns Adam, "you are doomed to die." Adam is from first breath a knowledgeable man, but being, as Augustine puts it, "unschooled in divine severity" (*inexpertus divinae severitatis*; *civ. Dei* 14.11), he still has much to learn about God's judgment. When he has to face that judgment directly, he becomes evasive. Augustine quotes him trying to foist his responsibility unto the woman and implicitly unto God (Gen. 3:12, translating from Augustine's Latin in *civ. Dei* 14.11): "The woman whom you gave to be with me, she gave to me, and I ate."

Augustine assumes an Adam who should have known better; otherwise the difficulty of Adam's life with the woman, lived outside a protected garden and in the wilderness of human history, will seem unjust—at best a case of parental neglect, at worse evidence of overt cruelty on God's part. But the crucial issue of just how deep Augustine takes Adam's knowledge to run proves terribly hard to resolve. What does Augustine's Adam really know, his evasions aside, about his own nature, his connection to the woman, his God?

Before Augustine gets around to discussing the human fall in *City of God*, a good chunk of which is devoted to Genesis exegesis, he takes up the case of angels and tries to account for why, at a time out of time, some angels, but not others, broke from the celestial chorus of divine praise, lost their spirit-tie to God, and morphed into agents of ignorance and confusion—i.e., into demons (*civ. Dei* 11.11, 11.33). At first he entertains the shaky hypothesis that the fallen angels, before falling, knew happiness with God but lacked the knowledge of whether they would forever endure in that happiness (*civ. Dei* 11.13). Their counterparts, the good angels, may have also lacked that knowledge, but they kept the faith. Alternately, these angels were, for some reason, gifted from the beginning with better knowledge. Either way, Augustine recognizes that he is close to giving uncertain angels a good motive for falling. If they cannot count on themselves or on God to be forever good, they may well be moved to seek security apart from their bond to God—although there is, as it turns out, no security there. Augustine's more considered opinion of the matter leaves him with two firm convictions and no better theory (*civ. Dei* 11.12, 12.6): he is convinced that no angel, no thinking being of any sort, can reasonably reject God out of a sense of lacking some good; he is equally convinced that the angels who are now in heaven have no fear of one day rejecting God without reason. The earthborn humans who are destined to join them have hope, his faith tells him, for the same security.

Between an angel and an Adam there is considerable difference. The angel lacks an original connection to flesh, knows nothing of flesh's parting and partnering, has no desire for mortal things. The angel that unaccountably sins turns from God and enters into a dark place of spirit, a place emptied of life and light. Augustine thinks of it as a second death (*mors secunda*; *civ. Dei* 13.1)—not soul's loss of body but spirit's loss of God. Although the human experience of sin has as much or more to do with the first kind of death, Augustine styles the angelic fall as the prequel to the human drama: know how an angel sins and you how an Adam does it as well. Augustine's emphasis here is on the stupidly self-aggrandizing impulse behind sin (*civ. Dei* 14.13, cf. 12.6). Adam has from God whatever he needs to be or become his desired self, and so does an angelic spirit, poised in heaven for a fall. When Adam and the angel who goes before him fall (feel free here to think of Satan), they begin to chase after a self they assume is more theirs than God's—as if God were the sort of creator to begrudge them their distinctive selves. They will chase after that self forever, never quite dying a second death. No originally living being loses the light of God entirely, but it is possible, Augustine believes, to take that light on a path of endlessly diminishing returns. Once on that path, there is no way off it—unless God intervenes.

Augustine does not expect God to intervene on behalf of Satan or any of the less famous demons; he faults Origen, perhaps the greatest theologian of the Greek East, for holding to universal redemption, God's love supposedly conquering all (*civ. Dei* 21.17). On this point he is not simply following Catholic dogma; he is sticking to his own logic of sin—the logic of absurdity. Demons do not sin because they succumb to an illusion of greater life, richer selfhood; they succumb to that illusion because they sin. It is the absurdity of their choice for privation over plenitude that moves them to concoct an illusion and follow it to hell. Apparently demons cannot bring themselves to believe that at bottom they crave privation; they have to believe something else. But even were they to be properly disillusioned (Origen imagines a cathartic hell), they would still have that absurd will to sin. The environment of choice is irrelevant. Return them to heaven or leave them in hell; their spirits remain tentative and fail to cling to God. When Augustine goes on to insist that the holy angels, having avoided a fall, become eternal clingers, he is changing the subject, not describing a transformation.

He is also changing the subject, but more deliberately, when he shifts from an angel to an Adam in his discussion of original sin. Augustine's Adam may seem at first absurdly demon-like in his decision to reject the peace and plenitude of Eden and follow his partner into sin (*civ. Dei* 14.10). But unlike a demon, Adam can be redeemed by a vision of divine flesh, gracefully rendered—a vision that he needs to "put on" (cf. *conf.* 8.12.29). It matters both to his sin and to his redemption that Adam is as much a creature of earth (the Hebrew meaning of *'adam*) as a son of heaven. When he is parted from his original flesh, he feels ecstatic (Gen. 2:23): "This one at last, bone of my bones and flesh of my flesh." Later he will feel vulnerable, her too (Gen. 3:7): "They knew they were naked, and they sewed fig leaves and made themselves loincloths." The capacity of flesh to join and part from flesh is a source of both ecstasy and vulnerability in human life; to know this and not shrink is to stretch into adulthood. Imagine an Adam who shrinks after a taste of knowing and resolves to live as if his flesh really were internally contained. Let his motivation be some combination of fear, faithlessness, and arrogance (but mostly the faithlessness). He will have cut himself off both from God, the breath of his breath, and from the woman, the ecstasy of his flesh.

The woman's role in Adam's crisis is ambiguous. Is she his co-conspirator in a crime against life, luring him to pit flesh against spirit? Or is she an agent of creation, inviting him to bring his share of spirit knowingly into flesh? Is she, in other words, taking Adam into his incarnation or moving him out of it? Can the answer sanely be both? She first enters the story when God puts Adam into a deep slumber, draws out one of his ribs, and fashions a whole from a part (Gen. 2:21–22). He awakens to find that he is both less and more than himself: he is a man related to a woman. She is bone of his bones, flesh of his flesh. That suggests either the most intimate of sexual intimacies or a mother's birthing of her son. The knowledge that Adam is being offered should help him sort out the difference. But something clearly goes wrong. Perhaps he takes too much to himself what he is mainly supposed to receive and care for. No son of God, after all, is ever born in Eden. That birthing has to wait, according to Augustine's faith, for a labor in time and history, where partialities are inescapable.

Augustine has trouble including woman in his image of the Trinity because she represents for him the love that exceeds itself and so leaves its recipient ecstatically—but also vulnerably—self-divided. Meanwhile God on high is supposed to be perfectly self-related and internally unaffected by his outreach to flesh. I am not suggesting that Augustine ought to have embraced a self-divided God; there are volumes of complaint to be lodged against such a notion. I am pointing out that the original sin of his Eve is far from obvious. Her taste of knowledge—a consuming that quickly becomes an offering—tests the law of divine desire. But does she violate it? Augustine evidently thinks so (*Trin.* 12.12.18), but he is the one who makes Adam out to be the only consensual partner to sin. The woman's offer to her partner of a knowing share in her life is an act that is either prior to sin or beyond it. Her motives, unlike Adam's, are hard to write off as veiled self-aggrandizement. Indeed she suggests through her offering the procreative alternative to sin: in place of self-consuming desire, we get the divine mystery of perfection without containment. Eve, "the mother of all that lives" (Gen. 3:20), aims to create not only with her partner, but also beyond him—and herself. Her mediation of divine knowing is to bring even death, or separation from life's source, into life's compass. If any of this can be believed, then the idea of a *procreative* transmission of sin is worse than nonsense: it is an invitation to refuse grace and render sin demonic.

Although Augustine holds tightly to his doctrine of inherited guilt throughout his long career as a bishop (he dies still defending it, *c. Jul. imp.*), he is never especially interested in working out the mechanism of transmission. His definitive discussion of the issue, four books on the soul and its origin (*an. et or.*), ends on an open note. Maybe the composite soul of everyone is amassed in Adam and gets divvied up, so to speak, through acts of procreation, or maybe it is the act that each time begets a wholly new soul. Augustine counsels Vincent, the impulsive young man whose craving for certainty occasions the need for the treatise, to "learn how not to know" (*disce nescire*; *an. et or.* 4.24.38). It is strange counsel if Augustine is so certain about sin's tie to procreation—in which case the first thesis, about the amassed soul, works best. But his investment lies elsewhere. He firmly believes that no son or daughter of Adam ever knows grace apart from what resists it. In that regard, Adam is in us and we are in him, facing once again the moment of Eve's offer. And the challenge will be to see it as a grace and not simply a temptation. When Augustine holds that contradiction together in his own person and gives it voice, he takes us to the scene of his conversion.

## CONVERSION

### The tie that unbinds

If a conversion, then from what to what? Augustine is already a convinced Christian at the outset of book 8, the book in the *Confessions* where he describes being able to heed, after much internal drama, a directive to "put on Jesus Christ" and "make no plans for the flesh based on lusts" (Rom. 13:14, translated from *conf.* 8.12.29). The lusts most at issue in book 8 are discredited things. They are dumb jokes, the vainest of vanities, old history. They tug pathetically at Augustine's tunic of flesh and try to beg him off the finality of his resolve (*conf.* 8.11.26): "You are sending us away? We will not be with you ever again from now to eternity; from now on and for all time, you will not be permitted this and that." This and that, *hoc et illud.* The confessing Augustine is too delicate, or perhaps just too prudent, to supply us with the referents, but his allusion is unmistakably to the sexual fantasies that keep him up at night (cf. *sol.* 1.14.25), even if they cease to rule his ambitions. Once upon a time he used to pray, "Give me chastity and self-restraint, but not yet" (*conf.* 8.7.17). Now he is ready to be relieved of unwanted desire and its outsized effect on his self-image (*conf.* 8.12.28): "One tomorrow after another—why not now? Why no end to my filth this very hour?"

Augustine's conversion, read along the lines I have suggested above, would be from a half-hearted resolve for a chaste life to a resolve that is fully determinative, but bizarrely impotent. Although there is something to this as a description of his internal distress, it makes for an underwhelming conversion. His view of his life's highest good will not have fundamentally changed, and he will be turning to God more for will-power than for wisdom: "Put on Jesus Christ, The Lord" (*induite dominum*)—an assumption of superior power and authority. I left out the title, *dominus*, when I first quoted the Pauline imperative that Augustine takes to heart. I introduce it belatedly in an effort to underscore the strangeness that gets introduced into that familiar honorific if Christ, as Lord, is really being "put on" to lord over and restrain Augustine's lusts. Is Augustine supposed to be gaining

Christ's power of self-restraint? As the wisdom of the flesh, the Adam who never sins, Christ has no need for such a power and is essentially alien to it (*nupt. et conc.* 1.11.13). There is nothing for Augustine to put on. But the pressing issue in book 8 is not, in any case, Augustine's need for sexual self-restraint. His lusts, he tells us, have already become the fading remnants of a misspent youth. They lack the power to drive him into the arms of another mistress. When he petitions for the highest kind of personal integrity (*continentia*), that of being at one with his better self, no more carnal residue, he is hoping to have his lusts eliminated altogether.

It is not abundantly clear why this is so important to him. If he is tempted by what he considers to be a lesser good or maybe even a base one, but he can resist the temptation, why is he so down on being tempted? An ineffectual desire for forbidden fruit can be like an inoculation; it boosts moral immunity by eliciting toughness of will. What Augustine describes in book 8, however, is more like his will's unraveling. He speaks of having two conflicting wills (*conf.* 8.5.10): one old and carnal, the other new and spiritual. His terms suggest his identification with spirit, but that is too simple. He is no more in his nascent love of spirit than he is in his departing lust for flesh. The reality is that he is self-dissociated and invested in conflict; this leaves him more the agent of his woes, but not wholly.

Augustine's recollection of his interior doubling or splitting is very complex. We need to attend to that complexity before we can have much of a sense of what was driving him to the brink. Here is a portion of what he remembers (*conf.* 8.10.22):

> Even as I was deliberating about how to serve my Lord God, as I had long been disposed to do, it was I who was willing; it was I who was not. There I was—not fully willing for, not fully willing against. And so I contended with myself and split me from me. The split was happening to me quite against my will (*invito*), not as a sign of an alien mind in my nature, but of my own mind, paying a price (*poenam meae*). In that respect, it was not I who was laboring to be self-divided but the sin living within me—the sin that is punishment for a freer sin. For I was a son of Adam.

When Augustine stops talking about his two wills as two antagonists and picks up with the notion of his two partial wills, locked into bad co-dependency, he changes the terms of what could count for him as resolution. If he is fighting an implacable foe, then he needs to win. If he is seeking to become whole, then he needs to be generous to the part of himself he finds most alien. Augustine invites us in the passage to think about Adam. When a distinct, still-to-be-known part of himself offers him knowledge, Adam faces a dilemma: he can either expend his love on the flesh of his flesh, or he can focus on his breath, his gift from God (Gen. 2:7), and try being whole alone. Either way he seems bound for a partial life. If Augustine finds that he lacks the know-how to knit breath and flesh together and still be a son of God, then more than inheriting Adam's punishment, he is facing Adam's problem.

The wisdom that Augustine remembers having before being thrown into crisis speaks to a conventionally philosophical piety. He knows better than to seek his life's worth from a high-profile job (he was, at the time, court orator in Milan), and he no longer has the burning desires he used to have for wealth and reputation. He is ready, *almost*, for retirement from the public eye and a contemplative life. Certainly he has the contemplative's disdain for the distractions of sex and family life. No less an authority than the Apostle Paul indulges the faithful in their need to marry (1 Cor. 7:8–9), but Augustine refuses to apply that indulgence to himself (*conf.* 8.1.2). He feels compelled to hold himself to a higher standard and do without the wife on his path to God. In the *Soliloquies*, a dialogue he imagines having with his own reason, his rational side wonders whether the lower standard is even a standard (*sol.* 1.11.18). It is one thing to turn to marriage to dignify sexual compulsion, quite another to expect that compulsion really to serve a higher aim. When Augustine assesses his prospects for spiritual uplift, he quickly notices what binds him most: "I was still being tightly knotted to woman" (*conligabar ex femina*; *conf.* 8.1.2). In other words, he is stuck in a bad marriage.

The Latin phrase I have translated as "to woman" is *ex femina*. As with the phrase, *ex nihilo*, the preposition, *ex*, signals a context of origin. God pulls materiality out of a void, *ex nihilo*, and simultaneously forms matter into the created order (*conf.* 12.29.40), of which human beings are a restless part. We are in some mysterious way still knotted to that original nothingness. It is not the cause of why we sin, but it is, Augustine suggests, the condition of sin's possibility (*civ. Dei* 14.13): "To be deformed by vice—that can't happen unless nature is made out of nothing." And then there is that other knot of human origination, common to Augustine and to every other son and daughter of Adam: being born of woman, *ex femina*. Just as he refrains from blaming the void for knotting his love to deformity, Augustine refrains from blaming women for forming deformity into an image of flesh and knotting his love to that. He blames his inner Adam.

As the one human being *not* born of woman, the outer Adam tried in his own way to rectify the omission. He chose Eve over God. However misguided his choice may have been at root, it is a more sensible, more seductive choice than turning from God and embracing the void. One is a choice of absolute death; the other a choice of mortality and a partial share in new life. In Augustine's mind there is an intimate and unavoidable connection between his entrance into the world *ex femina* and his Adamic desire for sex, for re-partnering. If woman were simply taken out of the picture, his tie to her undone (an unbirthing), then Augustine would be more angel than human in his temptations. Take away the void, the nothingness from which all things come, and there is no condition left for sin's possibility, either in heaven or on earth. There is only God, nothing else. It is not easy, while in the thick of a life's trial (*temptatio*; *conf.* 10.28.39), not to want to do away with too much. When Augustine turns Paul's practical counsel to the Church of Corinth—roughly, "Christ is about to return; don't get too preoccupied"—into a spiritual ideal of sexless Christianity (*b. conjug.*; *virg.*), he is arguably wanting to do away with too much.

But the usual complaint against Augustine is far more mundane, and it goes back to Julian of Eclanum, the Pelagian ex-bishop who saw in his nemesis a crypto-Manichean sex-hater. It is that Augustine misses or maligns the natural goodness of sex. Granted, it is possible to want too much of a good thing; it is also possible to want too little. Julian's Aristotelian alternative to a hyperbolic sexuality, given to lust and self-loathing, is a counsel of moderation (*c. Jul.* 3.13.27). In the right life, at the right time, in the right way, sex can express what is best about being human; it would be perverse and, God-forbid, Manichean to suggest otherwise.

The limitation of this healthy-minded moralism, when applied to Augustine, is that he could acquiesce to it without having much change for him. The quantification of sex—too much, too little, just right—is beside the point. Let married people have it just right; let abstainers stay humble and not think themselves superior. Augustine's root problem with concupiscence remains. Clearly he makes the problem out to be sexual in his own case, but more tellingly he never thinks of Adam as having stayed with Eve for the sex. The two of them, Augustine insists (*civ. Dei* 14.23–24), would have had perfect sex in Eden—rightly ordered, innocently pleasurable, and invariably fecund. Although he feels sure that sex is no longer like this, for anyone, he still wants us to stay open to the possibility that true ecstasy is not self-disfiguring.

If we hear him talking only about disfigurement, warning us that a sexual habit (*consuetudo carnalis*; *conf.* 7.17.23) clogs a life with unnatural heaviness, then all of Augustine's assurances about the hypothetically happy sex of a lost Eden will do nothing to make his theology seem less anti-sexual. The saintly life will be reduced in quick and dismal fashion to the sexless one—with God's help, no less. Christ will have descended to flesh to make a remnant of a saved remnant unusually chaste. He suffered and died on a cross for that? No doubt you can tell how I feel about this line of interpretation. What it misses is the very different sense that Augustine has of his own imperfection. He falls short of what he calls *continentia*—literally a state of being held together—not simply because he has desires that he does not want but because he is anticipated in all of his desires by an ecstasy that he cannot conceive. Not by himself.

Augustine did have a wife, not by law, but certainly in affection, and he tells us that he remained sexually faithful to her, his one woman (*unam*; *conf.* 4.2.2), during the years they were together. He does not reveal when he met her or where, or even her name, though clearly she was with him when in 371 he arrived for the first time in Carthage—"a frying pan of unsavory loves" (*conf.* 3.1.1). He was 17. Looking back he describes his adolescent relationship with her as a pact for having sex, not children (*pactum libidinosi amoris*; *conf.* 4.2.2). But they did conceive a child together not long into their history: the boy Adeodatus. The three of them remained in the same household until Augustine, now in his early thirties, established himself in Milan as a rhetor of some note, and Monnica, mindful of her son's future, arranged for his engagement to a girl too young to be wed but a good prospect for social climbing. The mother of his child returned to Africa, vowing never to be with another man. Augustine speaks of the effect on him of her departure (*conf.* 6.15.25): "My sins were multiplying all the while, and the woman with whom I used to share my bed, who was now an impediment to my marriage, was torn from my side; the heart in me, where once she was joined, was cut and wounded, trailing blood." His way of treating the wound of separation was to take on a mistress short-term, someone to tide him over until his fiancée came of age. This is not a pretty memory for him. He confesses that he was "a slave of lust" (*libidinis servus*) back then, not "a lover of marriage" (*amator conjugii*). And his lust, while allowing him to grieve "more coldly" (*frigidius*), was also making him more desperate.

His description of his separation from his partner, written to echo Genesis, occupies only a single paragraph in the *Confessions* (*conf.* 6.15.25). It is nevertheless an important passageway into the depths of his conversion, superficially his turn-about from pacts of lust to a stably celibate life of Christian service. While I don't wish to deny or belittle the surface conversion, I am also not going to pretend that it tells us much. The real story lies beneath the surface of his post-conversion celibacy. To get at those depths, we do not have to psychoanalyze him *in absentia*; we just need to pay close attention to his choices of wording, imagery, and scriptural allusion. The first Adam was originally parted from his partner without a wounding; that miraculous separation, also a joining, defined for him his marriage. Augustine describes a parting that is a wounding, and his efforts to rejoin himself to what he imagines having lost serve only to heighten his alienation. If we want a vivid sense of what it means to rely on lust (*concupiscentia*) when making plans for the flesh, Augustine gives it to us when he chases after the image of an image of a consummation. Sex with the short-term mistress fails to satisfy because she is to him only an image of the woman he has lost. His love, despite its veneer of lust, is more particular. But what has his partner been to him? His imagery makes her out to be an extension of his own body, like a graft of new flesh over his heart. In both cases, the images distort.

When he is parted from his partner—and his language indicates violence, not choice (*avulsa a latere meo*)—it is his pain that is his issue. He barely lets us notice that she has left him her son. Perhaps she did so because she loved Adeodatus and wanted him to have more opportunities in life. Perhaps she loved Augustine and wanted him to get to know his son better. Perhaps she loved them both and couldn't abide the thought of their separation. There are other possibilities, of course, most of them more cynical. From the little that Augustine says, one clear thing stands out about her: that his pact of lust with her was no longer (if it ever was) her pact with him. She walks away from the sexual partnership still his partner.

I am not telling you that Augustine was selfish and his woman a paragon of generous love. It is not for me to judge their ancient bones. But notice that if we read their love for one another cynically, making him Narcissus to her Echo, then the unity of their love reduces to a single, sensing body—his or hers, nothing other. And what can come of the one without the other? Take it from God, "It is not good for the human to be alone" (Gen. 2:18). We can try a less cynical reading. Suppose that Augustine's sexual appetite does not crowd out his grief quite as coldly as he would have us believe in his self-excoriation. Suppose that his woman—let's call her his wife—waits in faith for his healing without having to diminish herself or what she has been able to offer him. The more gracious possibilities suggest a different unity of love, impossible to grasp, but in place before anyone thinks to grasp at an object or an idea. It will always be too late for me to grasp a unity that runs "deeper than my depths, higher than my heights" (*conf.* 3.6.11). But I know that it is there when I have to give up a fiction of love's perfection, as I often do, and this leaves me feeling unexpectedly grateful and secure.

Augustine enjoys an unexpected feeling of security—he calls it a light (*lux securitatis*; *conf.* 8.12.28)—when he finishes reading the verse that directs him to stop making lust-based plans and trust in Christ: "Right when I got to the end of the verse, it was as if a securing light flooded my heart; every shadow of a doubt scattered." Soon after this he will tell his mother to forget about the marriage plans, more children, the business career. He is done with all that. His ridiculous old desires decisively behind him, he is ready for his baptismal rebirth. Only *continentia* is to be his wife from now on. Monnica is overjoyed (*conf.* 8.12.30).

And yet the most evident fiction in his conversion story surrounds the figure of continence—"serene and upbeat, but not crass, enticing me honorably," he recalls (*conf.* 8.11.27), "to come to her and not hesitate." She arrives on the scene in all of her allegorical splendor just before Augustine is completely at his wit's end. He has stopped listening to old habit, but he has yet to realize just how weak the resolve is that comes of that. She gently counsels him not to secure himself on his own but to fare forward and leave security to God.

With God as her partner, sublime Continence has brought many beautiful children into the world; none of them have birthed themselves. Why is Augustine, she wonders, so fixated on making himself the exception?

The matter that begs for consideration here is not the transparency of the fiction (that's patently obvious) but the reality that the fiction is meant to displace. Augustine's actual experience of *continentia*, both before and after his conversion, is nothing like his enticement by the fecund and unthreatening mother of his imagination. He testifies to a virtue that constantly has to fend off, like some ungovernable child, overly demanding flesh (*civ. Dei* 19.4). Even the best saints, and Augustine reluctantly adds Paul to the list (*c. ep. Pel.* 1.10.22; cf. *retr.* 2.1), have something carnal to repress. But if this is what continence is *really* like, what would move Augustine to let go of his fiction and get real? Though secured by God's light, he still finds himself having to repress what he wanted most to redeem. On the other hand, how can he continue to hold on to a fiction that has become so flimsy? He isn't getting any benefit from an imaginary continence; he can hardly expect to benefit more from the imaginary husband who would wed her.

There is another way to think about Continence in book 8, one that may allow Augustine a less fictional conversion. Suppose that the figure stands in for an actual woman and not for a virtue. The virtue is about strength of will and the shame of having to feel temptation. The woman is a part of Augustine's unmasterable past, but she is much more to him than just an embarrassment to his virtue. She shows him by her manner of departing that it is possible to be both self-possessed and self-giving. She leaves him her son, and this for her is no abrogation of a pact of lust; she vows never to lie with another man. Her self-possession apparently does not demand of her that she hold together all the parts of herself and never ungrip. She gives Augustine her share in the life they had together. It is up to him to know (or want to know) what that means. But since it is possible to read all kinds of motive—some fair, some foul—into her offering, he is likely to want a more reassuring gift. And so he invents Continence, the perfect wife and mother, to be God's counterpart. Now *those* are good parents; the son they would offer him would surely be an unmixed blessing. But now to the question: if he lets go of the fiction, will his reality be any better?

That depends on what we hear in the most famous passage of book 8, the one that many people, not especially obsessed with Augustine, love to cite. Augustine has left the side of Alypius, the friend keeping silent vigil with him in his garden retreat, in order to give way to a more private agony. He weeps uncontrollably under a fig tree and despairs of his future prospects. His past is too insistent, his God too angry. The passage picks up from there (*conf.* 8.12.29):

> Suddenly I hear a voice coming from a nearby house—hard to say whether it was a girl's or a boy's; it just kept chanting the words: "pick up and read; pick up and read" (*tolle, lege*). Right away I felt more relaxed, and I began to think hard about whether children use a chant like that in some game they play. But I couldn't remember ever hearing it before. My tears now in check, I stood up, convinced that the chant was nothing else than a divine command to me to open my book and read the first verse that comes to view.

It is striking that Augustine decides to accord a child's voice commanding authority. He knows next to nothing about this child, not even its gender, but its voice immediately diverts his attention. He unclenches. Up to this point he has been in volitional lockdown. Now he can will one thing: his willingness to be addressed. So far he gives us no reason to believe that a child is a likely figure of authority for him, much less a child playing a game. He isn't experiencing the child *per se* as authoritative. He hears the words, "pick up and read," and they remind of him of Saint Antony's conversion, how he had taken words not obviously addressed to him and heeded them as if they were. In Antony's case the words were from Matthew (Matt. 19:21; *conf.* 8.12.29): "Go, sell all that you have; give to the poor and you will have treasure in heaven; then come, follow me." When Augustine picks up his copy of Paul's letters (*codex apostoli*) and looks to find his life's imperative there, he is more likely to be thinking desert father than father of Adeodatus.

His son will die a few short years after his baptism, around the age of 17. Easter of 387 Adeodatus, Augustine, and Alypius are all baptized together in Milan, with Ambrose, the great bishop, presiding. We know from Augustine that Alypius looked into the same book that Augustine did, read one verse down, and found another imperative for

Augustine to follow (Rom. 14:1; *conf.* 8.12.30): "Take in the person weak in faith." Alypius was only too happy to think of himself as still weak and in need of formation if that meant being commended to Augustine's care. One can imagine, without knowing much about Adeodatus, that the boy felt similarly. For Augustine the timing of his baptism has had everything to do with his relation to an imperative to put aside his own unformed needs and put on Christ (Rom. 13:14). He must have met that imperative already having had some experience putting aside his needs. (If not, what was the boy's mother thinking, handing over her son?) He is due to get a great deal more as he settles into his life as the chief pastor of Hippo, a busy port city. But what about the putting-on-Christ part?

I have been urging a reading of Augustine's conversion that makes him less beholden to an ideal than to flesh-and-blood women. All the children of an idealized continence are themselves ideals. They are her perfected acts (*in omnibus continentia ipsa*; *conf.* 8.11.27), or perhaps they are the acts of her eternal husband; in either case, they stand in no particular need of parenting. Christ, having had a real human mother, was not like that. He came out of the womb an infant and with an infant's need of parenting. But being God, he converted that need into a virtue, a power to release his caretakers from servile need, more dispirited than animal, and freed in them their need for him. To put on Christ is to take on a burden of parenting and find it reassuring to learn that no parent who is not Christ, *dominus*, has ever finished growing up. We begin to parent the divine in one another when we are first helped to pull back from our most sterile desires. Such desires do not simply go away; they play into the tension that Augustine thinks of as a divinely parented life (*civ. Dei* 13.3): "We see that infants are weaker in the use and movement of their limbs and in their instinct for seeking and avoiding than even the frailest offspring of other animals, and it is as if the human life-force (*vis humana*) were elevating itself out of its own backwards impetus in order to excel over other animals all the more—just as out of a bow's bend, the arrow that is led back soars."

Augustine's conversion is not from lust to self-restraint. It is from murky self-preoccupation to the precise tension of a life consciously lived with others. That tension leaves him stretched between God and the void and tending toward God. He is confident of his direction not because he knows God or himself so well but because his confidence no longer depends on him having to secure his own knowledge.

There is an intimate kind of knowing that comes of that release, one more allied to trust than to desire.

### Learning a first logos

The light of faith, when it floods the heart, liberates perspective. Augustine stops reading himself into a world where he has no choice but to live his incarnation from the inside out, where his mortal frame defines the space that his soul inhabits. It is not that he will never again feel shortchanged and want what others have (lusts, in this life, don't go gently), but with God intervening between him and himself, he can no longer cozy up in quite the same way to his old desires. What he has come to see, and it seems to have been a sudden revelation for him, is that lusts—for him mainly "bedroom antics and indecencies, rivalries and wrangling" (Rom. 13:13; *conf.* 8.12.29)—do not parent flesh. They not beget or parent anything that is living and desirous of greater life. It was not lust that brought a child into Augustine's life and elicited from him his need to be a parent. His pact of lust with his wife in all but name had no provision for children: if they come, they come uninvited, and "compel themselves to be loved" (*conf.* 4.1.2).

Since most of us tend to think of lust as sexual lust—and then rate lust accordingly, depending on how we feel about sex—it is tempting, when reading Augustine, to equate his notion of lust with mere sex. But this way of reading him, assuming that "mere sex" makes sense, has him committed to confusing sin's appeal with sin itself. (He confesses to the confusion, but he is hardly committed to it.) Augustine firmly believes that no living being naturally loves losing life and lapsing back into nothingness; even suicides, he suggests (*lib. arb.* 3.8.23), wish to be free from pain, not from life. The appeal of sin, not being life's negation, must be something else. For Augustine that something else is either victory without cost (sin's hijack of will) or pleasure without labor (sin's hijack of appetite). There is nothing inherently bad about victory or pleasure; these are natural consummations, devoutly to be wished. But what does a perfect victory look like in this life? And how does a pure pleasure feel? Can we imagine these consummations ahead of time, and, if so, how well?

When Virgil has the imperial god Jupiter speak of a triumphant, final destiny for Rome, the associated imagery is of perpetual defeat, a kingdom defined by anger and loss. Behold the king of that kingdom (*Aen.* I, 293–296; Lombardo, 354–359):

The Gates of War,
Iron upon bolted iron, shall be closed,
And inside, impious Fury will squat enthroned
On the savage weapons of war, hands bound tight
Behind his back with a hundred brazed knots,
Howling horrible curses from his blood-filled mouth.

The victor, left out of the frame of defeat, is Augustus Caesar and his personification of the Roman imperium. It would take more than a poet's art to imagine him a victor victorious without cost.

The Augustine who confesses his hesitations about committing himself to the celibate life is already disillusioned with the ambitions of empire (*conf.* 8.1.2). He does not need to be convinced that an unrelenting need to win out over others, whether through war or war by other means, betrays a lust to dominate (*libido dominandi*; *civ. Dei* 1.1), the mark of a desperately unhappy will. He is not so convinced that his craving for pleasure, had with a partner, is just as suspect. But something changes in him over the course of his conversion. He becomes disillusioned. In *On the Good of Marriage*, a work not long to follow the *Confessions*, he does not limit marriage to child-bearing and the curbing of lust; "marriage is also good," he concedes (*b. conjug.* 3.3), "on account of the natural affiliation between the sexes." But certainly his more liberal readers will be sorry to learn that he has no hope for the sexual expression of that affiliation. "The better the marriage," he goes on to say, "the earlier husband and wife will have begun by mutual consent to hold themselves back from sexual commingling." He is not imagining two people hating sex and fleeing what they hate. There would be no merit in that, only necessity. He imagines two people disentangling their natural affection for one another from a hopelessly compromised good. When Augustine puts on Christ and accepts celibacy, he positions himself to be the best of husbands or at least an average monk.

As we know, Augustine ends up a priest, and by no means an average one, but this is not a direction that his sexual ethic would have dictated for him. His ethic reflects what remains unresolved for him after a lifetime's faithful struggle: how being a son of God frees him to be of mortal, mothered birth. His sexuality draws him powerfully into the mystery of his flesh but fails to illuminate it. His eternal, bodiless God fills his mind with light, but leaves his flesh to the darkness of desire. The taut pain of that tension—between wanting to know and wanting to be whole—is what finally steadies his will and, at the same time, humbles it. For Augustine does not will the conditions that shape his attention, and he does not will that to which he attends. Or as he himself puts it (*Simpl.* 1.2.10): "There are two things that God gives us: *that* we will and *what* we have willed (*ut velimus, quod voluerimus*). He wants the 'that' to be both his and ours—his by calling, ours by following. The 'what' he alone gives." The "what" is most basically a life. When his will becomes a conduit for divine light, Augustine is secured in his knowledge that his life, both spirit and flesh, is what he has been given to live. The flesh part of the offering continues to be hard for him, however, to want completely. In that, he is his own ambivalent Adam, bound for sexual trouble.

Was there ever a moment in which he felt unstretched and out of tension with himself? He never describes one. Not even the providential resolution of his agony in the garden, recounted more than 10 years after the fact, resolves him fully. He speaks there (*conf.* 8.12.29) of the security of his knowledge, not of his being: light illumines, doubts scatter, temptations persist. "Look!," he begs God a few books later (*conf.* 11.29.39), "my life is a stretch" (*distentio*). If we chart by the lights of Augustine's theology, we should not be so surprised that the stretch, more than the moment of illumination, is what counts. He lets us have our epiphanies on the road to Damascus or to wherever we assume, rightly or wrongly, that God is taking us, but these are negative revelations, insights into how blind we have been. Augustine gets his own version of a roadside revelation while trying to make sense of Romans 9: he is struck to his core by how deeply conservative and resistant to new life sin must be if, as Paul suggests, election is so gratuitous. Lust, Augustine is led to concede, is a universal solvent, not a sign of animation (*Simpl.* 1.2.20): "The carnal concupiscence that is sin's penalty now reigns, and it has reduced all of humankind to a single stew, where original guilt gets into everything." Happily the revelation of grace that moves ahead of this dark epiphany is more radical. Sin may be revealed in the moment, but grace has its roots in eternity. From where we stand, somewhere between the moment and eternity, the conjoined revelation feels like a stretch—and sometimes a pulling apart.

To get a better sense of what this stretch is, think of language-learning and its difficulties. Begin with a simple theory of teaching, the one that Augustine begins with in his treatise on scriptural interpretation, or how to become a good reader of the Word: "All teaching," he writes (*doc. Chr.* 1.2.2), "is either of things or of signs, but things are learned through signs." Say that I am trying to teach my young daughter, who is just beginning to use words, the meaning of the word pug. I point to the snoring mound of dog-flesh on the sofa (where no dog is supposed to be), utter the word pug, and hope that my daughter makes the intended association. Now add to this (overly) simple kind of teaching a theory of learner's motivation. What moves my daughter, what moves anyone to learn a language? If learning is more than conditioning (and let's assume that it is), then I can expect my daughter to become increasingly self-aware over the course of her initiation into a new language. At first her language-learning is probably much like conditioning. Out of an inarticulate desire to please her father, she pays attention to my gesticulations and the noises coming out of my mouth, and if the object that I am trying to get her to attend to is sufficiently diverting—it is cute, or curious, or colorful—she is moved, still in a largely inarticulate way, to associate her two forms of attention: to me and to the object. Years later, when she is able to move from her established word-use into new ventures of meaning, she will be articulating her motives for attending to things in quite sophisticated ways. What it means to her to please her father, to indulge the pug, to do the one in the context of the other or vice versa—all this and much more begins to emerge out of the inner life of her language-use.

Augustine is highly attuned to the goods that both direct and derail initiation into a language, and he suggests the following as a necessary principle of their inner ordering (*doc. Chr.* 1.3.3): "There are, on the one hand, things to be enjoyed, and, on the other, things to be used; some things turn out to be both." Now try to imagine a world of experience in which all goods are felt to have precisely the same valence: love of a parent, love of a child, a healthy diet, a great job, a dip in the pool, a fancy hair-do, all of these goods and countless others attract equivalently. If Augustine's principle is a valid and necessary principle, then your effort of imagining has ended in foreseeable failure. Let's be clear about what the source of the failure is. You can list a number of goods, as I just did, using the words you have learned for signifying them, and, in the abstract, you can think that all those goods have the same undifferentiated goodness. Of course you can do this. What you cannot do is play this game of abstraction without having to abstract yourself from the very practices of subordination, use to enjoyment, that have internally ordered your experience of goodness and allowed you your use of your words. It is only within a language that you can imagine yourself opting out.

But Augustine doesn't just want to claim that our expressive capacities are intimately bound up with our evaluative practices (that's a fairly uncontroversial thesis); he wants to weigh in on what those evaluative practices have to be. The only proper object of enjoyment, he insists (*doc. Chr.* 1.6.6), is the triune God—Father, Son, and Spirit; all other goods, make the list as long as you like, must be made subordinate to that one, sublimely enjoyable good. It is tempting, given our modern, post-Kantian ethical sensibilities, to hear him advancing an ethical theory, a very bad one. It is a theory that has us using and discarding non-God goods, like our neighbors, in order to get to God. Not very loving to the neighbors, to say the least, and not very loving of God to expect us to be like that. But to read Augustine this way is to assume, contrary to the deepest currents in his theology, that we have a neutral place from within ourselves either to sublime God or, more regrettably, something else. Go back to my language-learning daughter for a moment. Suppose that nothing ever emerges in her that craves a parent's recognition. Is she likely to learn a language, to develop self-awareness? I don't see how. When Augustine confesses that God alone is to be enjoyed (and his claim is essentially a confession), read him to mean that he owes his emerging self-awareness, the inner life of his language, to his craving for God's recognition and that alone. There is nothing to understand, no words to be spoken, apart from the Word that speaks from within the void and makes it fruitful. Such is Augustine's vision of language-learning.

Almost. If God is the parent of the logos, of language itself, then there is no end to the articulation of goodness. There will be always some further offering to pull us out of the womb of certainty and into the wilderness of abundant life; that is a stretch of our being in one direction. There is also the stretch the *other* way, not to an alternative intelligibility, a language of darkness, but to the illusion of one. It is a seductive illusion, and we cannot hope to see all the way through it in this life. But even to know as much that it is there, shadowing the logos, is no small achievement.

Augustine tries to elicit this knowledge from his son, Adeodatus, in the dialogue, *On The Teacher* (*mag.*), written less than a year before the boy's death and offering an accurate representation, Augustine later discloses, of the boy's gift (*conf.* 9. 6.14): "You know, God, that the views attributed to him there, as my partner in the conversation, were all really his." But the role of Adeodatus in the dialogue is not so much to advance a view, however intelligent, as to keep his father from claiming dogmatic authority for his. It is this use of his intelligence that is his true gift. (Here bear in mind that the Latin word, dogma, means teaching and that the name, Adeodatus, translates as God's gift.) Augustine opens the dialogue on a question of motive (*mag.* 1.1): "What do we seem to you to want to accomplish," he asks, "when we talk?" The question, raised by a father and asked of a beloved son, has a special resonance. This is not merely some abstract query about language-use. It invites recollection of the Trinitarian bond between Father and Son: a love so intensely generous it seems to add something even to God. It also hints at forgotten forgetfulness. Adeodatus gives his tentative response: "Inasmuch as I have an answer now, we want either to teach (*docere*) or to learn (*discere*)."

Augustine's next move, crucial to the underlying aim of the dialogue, is to press an unlikely thesis. He wants Adeodatus to drop learning as a motive for language-use. The only motive, he insists, is to teach, and to teach is to use a sign to evoke a meaning, the thing signified. I teach my daughter what a pug is when I use a spoken word, a picture, or a pantomime to get her to think of a pug. Augustine is indifferent as to whether to call this kind of teaching a reminding. (It seems more of a reminding once I can take her word-recognition for granted.) Again his main interest is to block learning. Even when it comes to asking a question, Augustine manages to find and make fundamental the dogmatic motive (*mag.* 1.1): "For I ask you this, whether you ask your question for any other reason than to teach the person you are asking what you want."

Adeodatus is never fully convinced of his father's dogmatism, but in one of the many ironies of the dialogue, he concedes to it without subscribing to a dogmatism of his own. His intent is to stay open to what his father may have still to teach him. But what is there to be learned from a conception of language-learning that makes a learner out to be so resolutely unreceptive? The lesson, at first, seems entirely negative. If we fancy ourselves teachers, skilled at affixing pieces of our inner life to material sounds and signs, all the stuff of incarnation, then we ought to take some time to notice how little we control the translation. Augustine presses hard on the basic insight that animates all of his reflection on teaching: that teaching aims at the thing to be taught, but always through a sign; the sign (*signum*) is not the thing itself (*res*). When my daughter uses the word pug, as I have taught her to use it, how do I know that she isn't using that word to mean what I mean by furry or sofa-loving or given to loud snoring? The tighter we tie language-use to the ghostly ideal of perfect translation, mind-to-mind, with the body acquiescing, the more painfully obvious it becomes that one life is closed off from another. The body never does acquiesce; its constant offering is to resist a certain pretension of spirit.

But I would not stay too long with a negative moral. The dialogue is not trying to convince us that we are at heart false teachers, stumbling over empty signs. How do I know that? I know it because the son still loves the father, even as the father affects to be the teacher he is not. (I have at times been both father and son.) Augustine and Adeodatus conclude that they do share an inner life together, one that neither of them possesses separately. They call this life their teacher. This is the life that both begins and ends their life's argument, allowing them learning through the hesitations, sometimes terrible, of sin. Augustine puts it this way (*mag.* 11.38). "The one who teaches, who is said to live in the interior person, where he is consulted, is Christ, God's unchangeable virtue and endless wisdom; every thinking living being consults this wisdom, but takes away only as much as it is able, according to its disposition (*voluntatem*), either good or bad."

Don't count on Augustine's Christ to be a mind-fixer. The power that bypasses a difference of flesh and fixes two minds directly upon the same thought—as comic as pug or as tragic as war—is no power of incarnation. It is really no power at all, but a disposition to resist wisdom, dressed as a conceit of learning. Remember that the only good to be enjoyed is God. And what is God? Nothing thinkable. Not completely. But neither is anything loved in the flesh completely thinkable. There is always something there that resists abstraction. Without that something there would be no grief, but also no beginning to a life—and so no new life.

"For there to be a beginning," Augustine writes (*civ. Dei* 12.21), "a human being was created, before whom there was no one." After Eden, there are beginnings still. No birth takes the sum of its measure from the previous Adam. It is Christ, as God, who parents the flesh; it is Christ, a mother's son, who brings to flesh a beginning—one in particular. The other beginnings are different. When Augustine puts on Christ, he does not become Jesus of Nazareth. He stretches, in a labor of incarnation, to accept who he is already in God's sight: a beloved son. No being not truly of the flesh can enter into the crucible of time's distension, self-divide, and emerge sanely different. I speak not of metaphysical alchemy but of genealogy. We were once the people who came before us, and now we are different. It all goes back to God—forward too. Augustine wants a life less pending (who doesn't?), but not a life apart (*conf.* 11.29.39):

> Now I spend my years sighing, while you, Lord, my solace, my father, are eternal. Still I am being scattered into times whose order I know not, and my deepest thoughts, my soul's viscera, are by happenstance and tumult being torn apart—until into you I flow, purified and made molten by the fire of your love.

## ALMOST AN EPILOGUE: TIME TROUBLED

*You cannot face it steadily, but this thing is sure,
That time is no healer: the patient is no longer here.*
                                                                    Eliot

Virgil ends the *Aeneid* with an unsettling image of triumph. Aeneas of fallen Troy, leader of a refugee people, has weathered shipwreck, unfated love, underworldly visions, and tribal warfare to find himself standing triumphant over a humbled Turnus, once a proud and unbending prince and now a suppliant. In a surge of rage, Aeneas refuses supplication and kills his helpless enemy, whose resentful soul slips into the underworld.

Turnus has done the most to make the fate of Aeneas a bloody one. The premise of the epic has been that Aeneas is destined to survive defeat, negotiate difficult seas (his odyssey), and settle finally on Rome's site, there to found a new empire out of Trojans and Latin tribesmen. He is sponsored in this fate, at times bullied into it, by Jupiter, the Olympian patriarch. But Jupiter does not invent the fate that makes for an Aeneas; that fate is in place before his involvement. Meanwhile the role of Juno, Jupiter's consort and rival, is to complicate the inevitable; she works to ensure that Aeneas pays a price, Jupiter too, for victory. Defying the sacred boundary between the realms of life and death, she lets a Fury out of hell to sow rumor, resentment, and rage among the peoples whom Aeneas would have otherwise won over quietly. More given to fury than most, Turnus feels the slight of being slighted all the way down to his depths, and he lets out his own bit of hell in a bid to claim his rights to a native throne.

Before all the fighting is done and he finishes a beaten suppliant, Turnus will have killed Pallas, son of Evander, a Greek king. Evander is the unlikely ally who puts Aeneas in charge of a leaderless Latin tribe and moves him a step closer to unified rule; he also entrusts Aeneas with educating his son in the art of war. When Aeneas looks down and sees that Turnus is wearing the ornamented belt of the slain prince, a grim trophy, he loses his composure and shows signs of a "savage grief" (*saevi doloris*). This leads to the epic's final slaying, set up as if it were a sacrificial offering (*Aen.* 12.947–952; Lombardo 1150–1157):

> "Do you think you can get away from me
> While wearing the spoils of one of my men?
> Pallas sacrifices you with this stroke—Pallas—
> And makes you pay with your guilty blood."
>
> Saying this, and seething with rage, Aeneas
> Buried his sword in Turnus' chest. The man's limbs
> Went limp and cold, and with a moan
> He soul fled resentfully down to the shades.

Turnus, it should be noted, never begged for his life; his petition was for his father, Daunus, who would need a body to bury before being able to consign his defeated son to beloved memory (*Aen.* 12.931–936; Lombardo 1129–1135):

> "Go ahead, use your chance. I deserve it.
> I will not ask anything for myself,
> But if a parent's grief can still touch you,
> Remember your own father Anchises,
> And take pity on Daunus' old age,
> I beg you. Give me, or if you prefer,
> Give my dead body back to my people."

We know what Aeneas ends up preferring, or what his anger has him prefer. He will be delivering a dead son back to an old man. Virgil gives us no reason to assume, given his characterization of his hero, that Aeneas will fail to deliver the body and choose instead to revenge himself or, as he says, revenge Pallas, on a corpse. This is the *Aeneid*, not the *Iliad*. So what is so unsettling then about the epic's final scene?

## ALMOST AN EPILOGUE

Not, I suspect, the mere fact of the murder. We can condemn it or condone it or take our reader's prerogative of suspended judgment—it is, after all, just a story. And it is a familiar story when retold at a comfortable level of abstraction: a powerful man, with a sense of destiny and some inner complexity, is prompted to remember that the bearer of his future—the heir he hopes will either perfect or surpass his self-image—has feet of clay; wanting to undo the memory, he strikes out in rage at its prompt, his external "teacher." In the particular version of this story that is his, Aeneas does not lose his own son, the boy Ascanius, surnamed Iülus (Julius), to the fortunes of war; he loses Pallas, one of his men. As long as he can substitute another man's son for his own—call this his sacrifice of memory, Aeneas can exit his story the presumptive father of an eternal kingdom, the Adam to an eventual Caesar.

But most of us know very well that time stands as silent witness against this conceit, both for the reader and for the fiction. At the end of a long song about "arms and a man" (*arma virumque cano*; *Aen.* 1.1), Virgil will have done less to canonize Aeneas, from the beginning a man of reverence (*insignem pietate*; *Aen.* 1.10), than to render him piety's question-mark. How is it possible to commend a sacrificed son to his father's memory and not invite more death into life? What does a lost future really ask of a Dido, of an Aeneas, of any reluctant prophet or hero? How do we let the future go and still have time ahead of us? No imperium, dreaming the dream of its own eternity, can afford to dwell on these questions, much less remember the answers.

As an augur for an eternal kingdom, Aeneas is remarkably bad at remembering. He affects to speak for Pallas, a lost son, cast into the underworld of a father's grief. We hear Aeneas speaking in the tongue of a moment's rage and impotence; he doesn't know in that moment the first thing about the love between a father and a son. He kills not to remember but to make the moment pass. Would he have had a better memory had it been Ascanius, not Pallas, whose voice needed retrieving from the underworld? What unsettles me most, I confess, is the thought that he would have. Virgil relieves me of my confidence that I can want a father, and not just some fiction of one, to mourn his son and not be angry. I admit it. I prefer eternal peace to piecemeal happiness. I want no parent ever to have to mourn a child. I want to live with my extended human family in the just kingdom that has no end. And until such time as that kingdom comes to pass, I prefer to do business with an angry God. (The forgiving one asks too much of my memory.) I am not as far from the reverence of an Aeneas as I generally like to imagine. He and his descendents, the Romans, all become great Juno worshippers, the goddess who remembers to be angry. Virgil, it seems to me, has not written an epic that is basically for or basically against empire; in those terms it is both and neither. He has more fundamentally tapped into the underworld of our human need for security. And things are very unsettling there.

There is no one in the ancient world more familiar with this unsettlement, more identified with it, than Augustine. Along with Virgil he gives it a literary form and even an itinerary, but no resolution. Still Augustine is no Virgil. He eventually breaks faith with his old literary love, the delight of his schoolboy days (*conf.* 1.13.22), and trades in Virgilian pathos for confessional self-scrutiny. No more weeping for Dido (*conf.* 1.12.21); Augustine weeps for sin. By the time he has begun the great work of his senior years, the formidable *City of God*, Virgil has become for him the honorary poet-in-residence of the dark city (*civitas terrena*)—a shadowy, often violent place where desire is opaque as earth and just as seductive.

Augustine is 59 when he writes the first three books of *City of God*. This is several years after Alaric marched his Goths into Rome and made that city seem less than eternal; it is about 2 years after the Conference of Carthage, where Catholic bishops in North Africa won imperial backing in their long struggle against their Donatist rivals. Marcellinus, sent by emperor Honorius to preside over the proceedings, was a close friend and disciple of Augustine's. He was hoping that in the wake of the Catholic victory Augustine would be able to persuade Volusianus, proconsul of Africa, to convert to Christianity. Volusianus was holding off largely because he was unconvinced that Christianity had been of more benefit to Rome than its ancestral pagan traditions (a commonly voiced skepticism of pagan elites, post Alaric). It is fair to say that imperial machinations and their churchly implications are much on Augustine's mind when he begins *City of God*, but as a work nearly a decade and a half in the making (he is 73 when he finishes it), it transcends its original impetus. The earthly city gets loosed from its initially tight association with Roman politics and history and, more particularly, with Rome's struggle, both helped and hindered by paganism, to keep love of legitimate glory from devolving into a lust to dominate (*civ. Dei* 5.19). In the abstract, the city becomes a dangerous ideal, a noxious prescription for peace.

The ideal is still Virgil's to articulate (*Aen.* 6.853, Lombardo 1018; *civ. Dei* 1.1): "To spare the humbled, and to conquer the proud." But the history of its implementation is hard to make out as anyone's: it's lust and domination, all the way down, or "love of self reaching into contempt of God" (*amor sui usque ad contemptum Dei*; *civ. Dei* 14.28).

One can imagine Virgil and Augustine, joined by David Hume and Edward Gibbon in some kind of celestial NPR round-table, having a spirited debate over the virtues of a pagan, as opposed to Christian, Rome. Only Virgil's position would be unforeseeable. Hume and Gibbon, both stylists of the modern age, would lament the replacement of paganism's vital passions with worship of the exclusive God, whose kingdom, in so far as it pertains to this world, sanctifies poverty and intolerance. Having devoted the first ten books of his massive opus to a blistering critique of polytheistically inspired justice and happiness (and the critique really doesn't end there), Augustine, I am confident to think, would disagree. But his disagreement would come with a qualification. The abstract distinction between an earthly city, hell bent on self-aggrandizement, and a heavenly city on earthly pilgrimage, honing its love of God, is easier thought than applied. "In this age," Augustine writes (*civ. Dei* 1.35), "the two cities are indeed thoroughly tied together and mixed in with one another; it isn't until the last judgment that they get separated out." Given that this age (*hoc saeculum*) comprises for him all of historical time, or time as we know it, the qualification seems big. Now we can never claim that some regime, some would-be empire, simply is the summation of God-contempt and stupid self-love; we would have to be living in hell to be able to claim that. Nor can we claim that some church of this age, calling itself Christ's and having arrived at some *modus videndi*, intimate or hands off, with secular power, just is all of God's city on earth.

Augustine's aversion to closure, whether claimed for the soul or the city, is one of the defining features of his theology. But there is more than one way to construe the aversion. The two I have in mind constitute a cross-roads for him. He cannot take one road without leaving the other behind, and he cannot move forward without choosing a direction. Most of the perplexity of his theology can be traced back to his tendency to linger or, what comes to same thing, to want to take both roads at once. One road is the path of belief, or, more accurately, belief in belief. On this path my Christian convictions won't necessarily make me a good person (indeed it would be both arrogant and naïve of me to think that they would), but they do define for me, in a way that I can fully understand, what the life is that is worthy of redemption. The fact that I see it but don't live it means that I am still laboring under a burden of unreasoning habit. I need grace to free me from my addictions and secure me in what I believe is most true. The other road leads to the underworld of belief: to unconfronted fears, forgotten desires, inarticulate hopes, lost innocence—all the stuff that must be ignored or repressed to have a perfect conviction. But this is not a path of disbelief or even suspension of belief. I don't move forward by negating or suspending a conviction that I have yet to perfect. And I do want to perfect my beliefs on this path. Call it a path of grace. Perfection on this path will require me to take a blessing, not a curse, from the underworld; it will always come in the form of a goodness that distends, sometimes wrecks my self's integrity. While in this life, I can never say when such blessings will end. And I know no other life.

Of course by calling one of the roads a path of grace and a path where belief is perfected, I seem to be suggesting that the other has no claim to grace and perhaps not much of one to belief. This is, in fact, exactly what I think. Still it is important that both roads be perceived to have some initial claim to grace and belief; otherwise Augustine's opting at times for both will have no seductiveness to it. And we would be fools to suppose that there is no seductiveness there. But now let me attempt to do the work of differentiation less ambiguously.

Consider the case of the Donatists. The Donatist movement had its roots in the Diocletian persecutions of the early-fourth century. Christians were required, on pain of death, to turn over their scriptures to Roman authorities for a public burning. The clergy who preferred compliance to martyrdom were known in the North African context as *traditores*—those who trade over (*trado*) their faith. Many North African Christians were convinced that the traditores had lost all authority to mediate the sacraments, including the consecration of priests and primates. In 313, when the deacon Caecilian was consecrated primate of Carthage by a suspected traditor, schism broke out. The suspicion was unfounded, as it turned out, but the divisiveness within North African Christianity continued unabated. One party took its name from Donatus the Great, the charismatic alternative to Caecilian in the See of Carthage, and it held its clergy to a rigoristic standard of sanctity. Donatists commonly thought of themselves as the church of the martyrs and were prepared to discount the Christianity of the more faint-hearted. The other party, championed by Augustine, claimed the mantle of catholicity for itself and emphasized outreach to a sinful world. The result would certainly be sin within the church, but the catholic side refused to believe that sacramental efficacy—the catharsis of a baptism or the validity of an ordination—depended on the sanctity of the officiant.

Around 408, still a number of years before the Conference of Carthage, where Donatists would lose all hope of a political victory, Augustine wrote to Vincent, the Rogatist bishop of Cartenna in Mauretania Caesariensis (*ep. 93*). An old acquaintance, Vincent knew Augustine from his bad old days in Carthage. Augustine opens reassuringly (*ep. 93* 1.1): "I am now more avidly in search of quiet than back when you knew me as a young man and Rogatus, your predecessor, was still alive." Augustine then goes on at length to give his reasons for why he and his fellow bishops are obliged, as pastors, to cooperate with imperial authorities in the suppression of North African Donatism. This was undoubtedly less reassuring to Vincent. The Rogatists were a Donatist splinter group, small in number and confined to Cartenna. They had repudiated the violent practices of some Donatist extremists (mostly a business of club-wielding gangs roaming the countryside), but they remained more aligned with a rigoristic ecclesiology than with the catholic alternative. Anticipating Vincent's objection that no one should be forced into righteousness (*cogi ad iustitiam*; *ep. 93* 2.5)—here meaning an upright Christian life—Augustine quotes what will become his favorite proof-text in debates over the propriety of religious coercion (Lk. 14:23): "Whomever you find, compel them to come in."

The context for that verse in Luke is the parable that Jesus tells of a great dinner, to which many are invited (Lk. 14:15–24). When the feast is ready to be served, the host sends his servant out to collect the invited guests, all of whom plead excuses for not coming. Basically they are too busy with their own wealth—new land, new oxen, new bride—to want to try out someone else's. When the host hears of this, he becomes angry and sends his servant out again, this time with instructions to go into the streets and alleys of the town and bring in the poor, the crippled, the blind, and the lame. It is easy to convince these people to come; they know that they could use a good meal. But their numbers fall well short of what the host's house can accommodate, and this is supposed to be a great dinner, to which many are invited. For a third and last time, the servant is sent out, now with instructions to return to the streets and alleys and compel whomever he finds there to come in.

This last directive, Augustine's proof-text, strikes me in its Lukan context as more perplexing than sinister. Is this a very big servant? How is he supposed to compel what is implied to be a large number of people to come to a feast for which they have no taste or hunger? I suppose, given the ease with which the needy people were brought in, that the best way would be to convince them that they are a good deal needier than they imagine themselves to be. But then Jesus ends the parable with the most perplexing line of all (Lk. 14:24): "For I tell you, none of those who were invited will taste my dinner." The servant in the story is no longer being addressed ('you' is plural in the Greek); Jesus has reverted to his own role as host and is now speaking to his audience, who is there, along with him, dining on some other host's lesser fare (Lk. 14.1). What perplexes me most about his concluding line, the moral of his parable, is its implication that the poor, the crippled, the blind, and the lame aren't on the messianic guest list. I get it that the original invitees won't be coming; they are too tied to the riches of this world to want something more. The poor and company are coming, but not, it would seem, because of the neediness that they perceive in themselves. (The prodigal son thought he was needy too, but this is not why he ended up fêted at his father's house.) So I wonder: why isn't our self-confessed neediness our ticket into the banquet hall of God's city?

I have learned from Augustine, the great student of grace, to value this kind of question, but he asks himself nothing of its like when he adapts Luke to Realpolitik. The servant in his version of Luke's parable is the servant church, called especially to gather the humbled to the Lord's table and to rebuke the proud. When this church comes head to head with its own animus, that of the self-admiring servant, lacking in humility, it cannot be content merely to rebuke. It must end its self-division and compel unity. The means of compulsion, Augustine concedes, should be moderate. No torture or capital punishment, but fines, confiscation of property, and exile are all within the bounds of the permissible (*ep.* 93 3.10). The Donatists are to be given a lesson, it seems, not about the agonies of the flesh, but about its persistent vulnerability to poverty and so about its inherent neediness. Threaten to take away their material sustenance with a strong imperial hand, and they will soon break with their empty habit of casting themselves a people apart. Augustine has seen the results. His own native Thagaste, once a Donatist enclave, went Catholic "out of fear of the imperial laws" (*ep. 93* 5.17), and now no one is complaining. It is cases like that, Augustine confides to Vincent, that finally changed his mind about compelled catholicity. He used to be against any kind of compulsion in matters of faith. But who can argue with results?

My point is not that Augustine surely must have been deceived about the good people of Thagaste and elsewhere; nor am I suggesting that he had no justification for wanting to mix some imperial politics into his church affairs. The church and the earthly city, being part of the same admixture, are bound to aspire to peace in roughly the same way: forge or force agreement out of a conflict of wills. The forging is not always so different from the forcing. Obvious tyrants rule from fear; the more subtle ones appeal to freedom and get people to tyrannize themselves. As any thinking creature of appetite is liable to discover, forces of desire can be divisive in the most stable of marketplaces: some people will be served more than others, some far more, some not at all. The pursuit of happiness commonly divides us, one from another. Still if the veneer of peace that gets pasted over all this is a universal good—as Augustine seems to think ("there is no one who does not want to have peace"; *civ. Dei* 19.12)—then his reasons for giving into a limited coerciveness may lie somewhere within the paste: in the admixture of fear and desire that both conditions and limits consent (cf. *spir. et litt.* 31.53). I would be a hypocrite to deny him that possibility; I too value the peace of the earthly city—no doubt to a fault. But I would urge against him, with the student of grace as my ally, that there is no spiritual use to be made of a coerced peace. None, at least, that avails itself to human calculation.

When Augustine assumes otherwise, he lapses into bad analogies. There is a striking instance of this in his letter to Vincent, where he compares God the Father to Judas Iscariot (*ep. 93* 2.7). Augustine is quite prepared to condemn Judas for having turned Jesus over to the Sanhedrin and by extension to the Roman imperium. But Augustine also believes, on Paul's authority (Rom. 8:32), that God too can be said to have handed Jesus over. "In regard to this handing over (*hac traditione*), why," asks Augustine, "is God holy and the man guilty, if not because there was no one motive (*causa*) for the one thing they did?" The question, which contains its own answer, is doubly misleading. First of all, Judas and God don't really commit the same act. Judas creates a void in the good by acting out of fear and greed; God creates goodness out of a void by stripping fear and greed of their authority. It isn't Judas who will determine the meaning of the crucifixion. But having locked God and Judas into the same act of betrayal, Augustine finds that he can exonerate God only through a difference in motive. And this is what is most misleading about his rhetorical question. He encourages Vincent to focus on the wrong kind of difference.

Imagine a less greedy Judas. He does not betray Jesus for the money. He genuinely believes that his teacher, whom he has come to love, has become a danger to his own people. Too many Jews falsely assume that Jesus is going to free them from Roman occupation; that assumption is more than likely to get most of them killed. For the sake of the greater good, Judas very reluctantly and with great internal torment decides to hand Jesus over. Does the difference in motive mitigate his guilt? Just on basic considerations of justice alone, I think that it would have to. But now take the next fateful step and try not to notice the theological abyss yawning before you. Imagine Judas having God's motive for having turned Jesus over. Is he now guilt free? He would be if it were possible to reason like this: if an act that I do wickedly is an act that God can do well, then I can do that same act well as long as I act with God's intent. In other words, I just have to anticipate and then will the good that God would be bringing to my situation.

With some charity, we can leave Augustine with juridically respectable reasons for having preferred imperial intervention to civil unrest. But we do him no service at all if we concede to his church anything remotely like this power of anticipation. The core insight of his theology is that God sets *all* of the conditions for grace, including the need. We can add as much nobility as we can possibly muster to our coercive practices; we still will not be able to prompt in others or in ourselves the need for grace. Any church that denies or forgets this ceases to refer its virtues to God (*civ. Dei* 19.25). Soon it will find itself embracing the same imperatives that define the earthly city: spare the humbled, beat down the proud.

When Aeneas first hears of these imperatives, Virgil has him in the underworld, listening to the shade that was in life his father, Anchises.

## ALMOST AN EPILOGUE

Here is the fuller directive that passes from father to son in that most unlikely of places (*Aen.* 6.847–853; Lombardo 1012–1018):

> Others will, no doubt, hammer out bronze
> That breathes more softly, and draw living faces
> Out of stone. They will plead cases better
> And chart the rising of every star in the sky.
> Your mission, Roman, is to rule the world.
> These will be your arts: to establish peace,
> To spare the humbled, and to conquer the proud.

It is not hard to hear in the passage the beginnings of a confusion between the art of peace-making and imposed rule. Perhaps the confusion for citizens of the earthly city is, as Augustine suggests, as unavoidable as sin itself. (We live still in the shadow of that one unfinished transgression.) Students of the earthly city and mythologists of empire would nonetheless do well to keep in mind the underworldly context of Virgil's nascent imperialism.

Aeneas is not being given sunlit imperatives to apply without a moment's cost to the world of the living, where death is more a fear than a wisdom. He is taking his share of the underworld with him to his new home. It dogs him like a Fury when he denies it. When he kills Turnus, he seems more Fury than man. He has lost his ability to discern the difference between pride and humility. The man kneeling before him, pleading for a father's memory, is apparently not reminder enough. The Fury reemerges, and Aeneas can see only a rival victor at his feet, playing at suppliant. He dispatches the threat and pays Juno's ultimate price—and Rome's—for victory. Virgil's Juno, the goddess most in touch with the power of the underworld, is quite clear about what that price is. She will end her efforts to subvert the will of Jupiter, her sky-dwelling consort, on one condition (*Aen.* 12.828; Lombardo, 999–1000): "Troy has fallen. Let the name of Troy be fallen too." Jupiter foolishly agrees and assures her that when it comes to the Romans, "no nation shall be more zealous in Juno's worship" (*Aen.* 12.840; Lombardo 1014–1015).

The gods give Aeneas his victories, but not his life. His torment is that he cannot remember the importance of that difference. He doesn't remember what it means to have been a Trojan and the young son of a living father. His final act in his own drama is to offer blood to the angry shade that has displaced his memory. There is no reverence there. If I were to write the epilogue for Aeneas the pious, his epitaph too, it would go something like this:

> Once upon a time, I was a wandering Aeneas, feeling victimized by an angry goddess. (She cost me a good marriage and an ordinary life, among other things.) A living man once told me that I would have to love and worship this goddess above all others; a dead man once told me that I'd father a race of conquerors. I put the two wisdoms together when I killed a man who bore for me the image of my own impotence. From then on, I learned to love righteous anger. I learned to love Juno, and I no longer wandered—for every land was my own.

I'll always wonder what Virgil himself would have written. The received tradition on the *Aeneid* is of a hauntingly unfinished poem. Virgil completed a draft but became mortally ill before he could undertake the revisions. According to one of his ancient biographers, he wanted the manuscript burned upon his death, but Augustus Caesar intervened. A better poet for Augustine's earthly city and all its ambiguities can scarcely be imagined.

But what of the other city, more other than under in its worldliness, and what of its restless theologian? "You stir us and we delight to praise you, who made us yours—and so the heart within us is restless until it rests in you" (*conf.* 1.1.1). This is the psalm of the celestial city on pilgrimage. In its anticipation of life with the angels (*civ. Dei* 12.1), it is a city that travels light and aims high; all the heaviness of the trip derives from the mysterious entanglement of above with below, of heaven with earth. I say mysterious because it is not clear that such entanglement is even possible. What does a death or a birth really have to do with a life that's eternal? Augustine tries to take credit for the mystery (he calls it the blame) when he owns up to his sin and that of Adam before him. But his God dispossesses him of his defeats as readily as his victories and gives him his life. He is himself the mystery of entanglement, but not its cause. The question for him and for every other citizen of the two cities, become one in this life, is whether a life is ever received in the possessing. The restless theologian suggests not. He wants to give his heart back, and, by giving it back, he hopes to keep it.

Naturally I would like to know, as one of those dual citizens, whether Augustine's kind of restlessness is ever resolved. But this is like asking for an epilogue to time itself. Augustine almost gives one, or a promise of one, when he tries to imagine what time looks like from God's point of view (*conf.* 11.31.41):

> If a mind is equipped with so great a knowledge and prescience that all things past and future are known to it, as, say, a very familiar psalm is known to me, then certainly this mind is a marvel beyond measure, stupendous to the point of inspiring awe. To such a mind nothing of the ages is hidden, nothing done, nothing remaining to be done, just as when I am singing that psalm, it isn't hidden from me how much of the psalm I have sung, how much I have left to sing. But perish the thought that you, the creator of the universe, the creator of souls and bodies, know all things past and future this way. Your way is by leaps and bounds more marvelous and more hidden.

Augustine has here refused himself the consolation of an analogy. He will not let those brief times when he feels at one with his knowing shape his expectation of the divine intelligence. But why not? What's the harm? Granted, when he is singing a familiar psalm, his mind is still distended; his awareness has to reach back into what is no longer and forward into what is not yet. If the time covered remains relatively short, however, his mind need not distend much. Augustine, signing a psalm, is hardly the paradigm of an agonized consciousness, distending into non-being. On the other hand, how odd that I should think this. I must have forgotten what a psalm is and why Augustine likes to sing them. I can, of course, now try to make a virtue out of my flattened perspective. It doesn't matter, I insist, what the *content* of Augustine's memory is. All that matters is that the thing to be remembered be brief. Let him be singing a child's ditty or reciting his ABCs. Anything trivial and short will do. But now notice. The closer I bring God to a mildly distended human mind, the more I am driven to trivialize my human awareness of time. I cannot be thinking about life and death, good and evil, when I have time only briefly in mind. Augustine is right. Not only am I nowhere near the mystery of God's time; I am running in the other direction. I am running by leaps and bounds away from incarnation.

Augustine's refusal of the comfort of analogy is the great refusal of his theology. He embraces a mystery in order to avoid falling for a lie. The lie is that he is most himself when he is nearest a self-contained intelligence. The mind that took in all of time and made it seem like a psalm—albeit without the quality of praise—for a moment looked divine to him. It was almost an epilogue, but not quite. Thank God.

# SUGGESTED READINGS, CHAPTER BY CHAPTER

## CHAPTER ONE

### A heritage transformed

Cochrane, Charles Norris. *Christianity and Classical Thought: A Study of Thought and Action from Augustus to Augustine.* Rev. edition. New York: Oxford University Press, 1944. [An argument for thinking of Augustinian Christianity as a radical reformulation and critique of classical philosophical ambitions.]

Herdt, Jennifer A. *Putting On Virtue: The Legacy of the Splendid Vices.* Chicago: University of Chicago Press, 2008. [Habitation to virtue is an Aristotelian notion that Augustine calls into question. Herdt offers a judicious assessment of the nature, limitations, and legacy of the Augustinian critique.]

Marrou, Henri-Irénée. *Saint Augustin et la fin de la culture antique.* Paris: E. De Boccard, 1938; *Retractatio* [A reconsideration]. Paris: E. De Boccard, 1949. [Marrou struggles to determine whether Augustine's transformation of classical paideia is primarily the story of an ending or a beginning.]

Pollmann, Karla and Vessey, Mark, ed. *Augustine and the Disciplines: From Cassiciacum to Confessions.* New York: Oxford University Press, 2005. [Essays that explore Augustine's debt to and departure from the liberal arts; the introduction is especially helpful.]

Wolterstorff, Nicholas. *Justice: Rights and Wrongs.* Princeton: Princeton University Press, 2008. [Wolterstorff argues forcefully that Augustine breaks from classical fixation on happiness—a sea-change in the history of philosophy; see pp. 180–206.]

### Stoicism in Augustine

Colish, Marcia. *The Stoic Tradition from Antiquity to the Early Middle Ages.* Volume II. Leiden: E. J. Brill, 1985. [The best exposition of the sum of Augustine's Stoic borrowings.]

Sorabji, Richard. *Emotion and Peace of Mind: From Stoic Agitation to Christian Temptation.* New York: Oxford University Press, 2000. [Sorabji casts Augustine as an influential misreader of Stoicism; see especially pp. 372–384.]

## Death and grief

Cavadini, John. "Ambrose and Augustine *De Bono Mortis.*" In *The Limits of Ancient Christianity: Essays in Honor of R. A. Markus.* Ed. William Klingshirn and Mark Vessey. Ann Arbor: University of Michigan Press, 1999, pp. 232–249. [Cavadini makes salient Augustine's sense of the evil of death, the contrary pull of a Christian Platonism notwithstanding.]

Helm, Paul, "Augustine's Griefs," and Wolterstorff, Nicholas, "Suffering Love." Both reprinted in *Augustine's Confessions: Critical Essays.* Ed. William E. Mann. Lantham: Rowman & Littlefield Publishers, 2006, pp. 147–160 and pp. 107–146 respectively. [A contrast of perspectives.]

Pagels, Elaine. *Adam, Eve, and the Serpent.* New York: Random House, 1988. [Pagels sympathizes with the Pelagian attempt, contra Augustine, to naturalize death and remove its stigma of punishment; see pp. 127–150.]

## Augustine and Cicero

Foley, Michael. "Cicero, Augustine, and the Philosophical Roots of the Cassiciacum Dialogues." *Revue des Études Augustiniennes* 45 (1999) 51–77. [Foley's well-argued thesis is that Augustine styled his early dialogues, written at Cassiciacum, as responses to a Ciceronian paradigm—with one exception.]

Graver, Margaret. *Cicero on the Emotions: Tusculan Disputations 3 and 4.* Translation and Commentary. Chicago: University of Chicago Press, 2002. [Graver does not bring Augustine into her commentary, but her treatment of Cicero is quite relevant to Augustine's understanding of emotion, grief especially.]

Testard, Maurice. *Saint Augustin et Cicéron.* 2 vols. Paris: Études Augustiniennes, 1958. [Still the classic exposition of Augustine's Ciceronian borrowings.]

## Augustine and Pelagius

Bonner, Gerald. "Augustine and Pelagianism." *Augustinian Studies* 24 (1993) 27–47. [A summary account of the development of Augustine's anti-Pelagian theology, but also a critique.]

Brown, Peter. "Pelagius and His Supporters: Aims and Environment." *Journal of Theological Studies* 19 (1968) 93–114. [Brown has a compelling sense of Pelagianism's classical pedigree.]

De Bruyn, Theodore, trans. *Pelagius's Commentary on St Paul's Epistle to the Romans.* Oxford: Clarendon Press, 1993. [In his commentary Pelagius appears to be familiar with Augustine's forays into Romans, most notably his responses to Simplician. From a Pelagian point of view, Augustine goes off the deep end when he reads Paul to be suggesting that guilt is heritable and election gratuitous. Pelagius avoids similar "errors" in his own commentary.]

## Augustine's Manicheism

Brown, Peter. *Augustine of Hippo: A Biography*. New edition. Berkeley: University of California Press, 2000. [The chapter on Manicheism is an extraordinary offering in an extraordinary book; see pp. 35–49.]

Clark, Elizabeth. "Vitiated Seeds and Holy Vessels: Augustine's Manichean Past." In *Ascetic Piety and Women's Faith: Essays on Late Ancient Christianity*. New York: Edwin Mellen, 1986, pp. 291–349. [A brilliant assessment of Augustine's crypto-Manichean ambivalence toward reproduction, following the lead of Julian of Eclanum, Augustine's great late-in-life antagonist.]

## CHAPTER TWO

### The will

Arendt, Hannah. *Willing*. Volume Two of *The Life of the Mind*. New York: Harcourt, Brace, Jovanovich, 1978. See pp. 84–110: "Augustine, the first philosopher of the Will." [Arendt, a great philosopher in her own right, is one of Augustine's best readers.]

Dihle, Albrecht. *The Theory of Will in Classical Antiquity*. Berkeley: University of California Press, 1982. See pp. 123–144. [Dihle stresses Augustine's conceptual innovation.]

Harrison, Simon. *Augustine's Way into the Will: The Theological Significance of De Libero Arbitrio*. Oxford: Oxford University Press, 2006. [In a close reading of Augustine's most analyzed early work, Harrison associates the will with the irreducible integrity of a first-person point of view—an exercise of the Augustinian cogito.]

Kahn, Charles. "Discovering the Will: From Aristotle to Augustine." In *The Question of "Eclecticism": Studies in Later Greek Philosophy*. Ed. J. M. Dillon and A. A. Long. Berkeley: University of California Press, 1988, pp. 234–259. [Augustine innovates by way of his theological concept of will, but on Kahn's account he is more bricoleur than magician.]

### Evil

Evans, G. R. *Augustine on Evil*. Cambridge: Cambridge University Press, 1982. [A survey of Augustine's evolving sense of the problem of evil.]

Mathewes, Charles. *Evil and the Augustinian Tradition*. Cambridge: Cambridge University Press, 2001. [In terms of metaphysics, evil is a privation of goodness; psychologically speaking, it is more a perversion. Mathewes plays out these two sides of Augustine's theory of evil in twentieth century Augustinianism. Hannah Arendt and Reinhold Niebuhr figure prominently.]

## Augustine and Plotinus

Cary, Phillip. *Augustine's Invention of the Inner Self: The Legacy of a Christian Platonist.* Oxford: Oxford University Press, 2004. [Cary notices an unresolved, perhaps irresolvable, tension in Augustine between his Platonically inspired interiority and his devotion to Christ. The thesis is not new, but Cary's development of it is.]

Courcelle, Pierre. *Recherches sur les Confessions de saint Augustin.* Paris: E de Boccard, 1950; expanded edition, 1968. [A landmark study, shaping decades of scholarship on Augustine's Platonism; Courcelle makes the case for the interpenetration of Christian and Platonist intellectual culture in Milan, where Augustine met up with Ambrose and his circle.]

Kenney, John Peter. *The Mysticism of Saint Augustine: Rereading the Confessions.* London: Routledge, 2005. [The best recent account of Augustine's contemplative theology; the pagan Platonism of Plotinus serves as foil.]

McGroarty, Kiernan. *Plotinus on Eudaimonia: A Commentary on Ennead 1.4.* Oxford: Oxford University Press, 2006. [A treatise that comes late in the life of Plotinus; it supplies an apt entry into the ethics and metaphysics that liberated Augustine from his materialism.]

Menn, Stephen. *Augustine and Descartes.* Cambridge: Cambridge University Press, 1998. [Don't let the title deter you; Menn offers a detailed and illuminating analysis of Augustine's reception of Plotinian metaphysics, especially its notion of Mind. Note especially pp. 185–206, the section on "Christianity and Philosophy."]

Rombs, Ronnie J. *Saint Augustine and the Fall of the Soul: Beyond O'Connell and His Critics.* Washington, D. C.: Catholic University Press, 2006. [Both a well-tempered assessment of Robert J. O'Connell's controversial reading of Augustine's debt to Plotinus and a good introduction in its own right to Augustine's Platonism.]

## Time and memory

Cavadini, John. "Time and Ascent in *Confessions* XI." In *Augustine: Presbyter Factus Sum*, ed. J. Lienhard, E. Muller, R. Teske. New York: Peter Lang, 1993, pp. 171–185. [Cavadini's Augustine is less ambivalent than Marrou's (see below) about the goodness of time.]

Marrou, Henri-Irénée. *L'Ambivalence du temps de l'histoire chez Saint Augustin.* Montreal and Paris: Librairie J. Vrin 1950. [Still the classic account of Augustine's ambivalent valuation of historical time.]

Matthews, Gareth. "Augustine on Reading Scripture as Doing Philosophy." *Augustinian Studies* 39.2 (2008) 145–162. [The scriptural text at issue is the first verse of Genesis. Matthews follows Augustine into a detailed meditation, exegetical and philosophical, on the divine creation of time.]

## Augustine and Petrarch

Gill, Meredith J. *Augustine in the Italian Renaissance: Art and Philosophy from Petrarch to Michelangelo.* Cambridge: Cambridge University Press,

2005. [Includes a fine discussion of the Augustinian moment in Petrarch's ascent of Mount Ventoux; see chapter three, "Petrarch's Pocket," pp. 99–111.]

## CHAPTER THREE

### Augustine and sexuality

Brown, Peter. *The Body and Society: Men, Women, and Sexual Renunciation in Early Christianity.* New York: Columbia University Press, 1988. [See Chapter 19, pp. 387–427. Brown situates Augustine's struggle for sexual continence within the context of late antique asceticism.]

Cavadini, John C. "Feeling Right: Augustine on the Passions and Sexual Desire." *Augustinian Studies* 36:1 (2005) 195–217. [A daringly provocative rehabilitation of Augustine's portrait of passionless sex in Eden. This essay is becoming something of a classic among Augustine scholars—particularly the ethicists.]

Lamberigts, Mathijs. "A Critical Evaluation of Critiques of Augustine's View of Sexuality." In *Augustine and his Critics*. Ed. Robert Dodaro and George Lawless. London: Routledge, 2000, pp. 176–197. [Mostly focused on Julian's critique of Augustine's obsession with concupiscence, but mindful of modern sensibilities as well.]

Power, Kim. *Veiled Desire: Augustine on Women*. New York: Continuum, 1995. [A comprehensive survey of what Augustine wrote about women, laced with psychological and anthropological analysis.]

### The unnamed partner

Danuta, Shanzer. "Avulsa a Latere Meo: Augustine's Spare Rib." *The Journal of Roman Studies* 92 (2002) 157–176. [An essay on the allusiveness of Augustine's Latin in *conf.* 6.15.25. The play on and against Gen 2:22–24 is showcased. I owe a great deal to Shanzer's reading.]

Miles, Margaret R. "Not Nameless but Unnamed: The Woman Torn from Augustine's Side." In *Rereading Historical Theology: Before, During, and After Augustine.* Eugene, Oregon: Cascade Books, 2008, pp. 127–148. [A sober assessment of what we can claim to know about the mother of Adeodatus—not her subjectivity.]

### Conversion

Fredriksen, Paula. "Paul and Augustine: Conversion Narratives, Orthodox Traditions, and the Retrospective Self." *Journal of Theological Studies* 37 (1986) 3–34. [Augustine tells the story of his conversion more than 10 years after the fact, and he draws on exegetical and existential perspectives he simply could not have had at the time. Fredriksen helps us think through the implications of this. Aside from its illumination of Augustine in particular, her essay is a contribution to a philosophy of historical reconstruction.]

James, William. *Varieties of Religious Experience*. [The classic work that continues to shape much of the contemporary debate over the experiential dimensions of the religious life. James, like Augustine, suggests two, superficially conflicting models of conversion: the quick flash in the soul of a transforming insight and a lifetime's labor in virtue.]

Turner, Denys. *The Darkness of God: Negativity in Christian Mysticism*. Cambridge: Cambridge University Press, 1995. [A good antidote to the notion, disastrous when applied to Augustine, that mystical consciousness depends on having a certain, ineffably sensational kind of experience.]

Wills, Garry. *Saint Augustine's Conversion*. New York: Viking Penguin, 2004. [Wills translates book 8 of the *Confessions* with his usual panache and adds a commentary, much of it directed against "the myth of suddenness."]

## Paul in Augustine

Burns, Patout. *The Development of Augustine's Doctrine of Operative Grace*. Paris: Études Augustiniennes, 1980. [A patient exposition of Augustine's unfolding sense of how grace works; much of the development passes through Paul.]

Fredriksen, Paula. *Augustine and the Jews: A Christian Defense of Jews and Judaism*. New York: Doubleday, 2008. [Part Two of this book, "The Prodigal Son," weaves together Augustine's readings of Paul, Romans especially, into a narrative of his theological coming of age.]

Stendahl, Krister. "The Apostle Paul and the Introspective Conscience of the West." In *Paul Among Jews and Gentiles*. Philadelphia: Fortress Press, 1976, pp. 78–96. [Augustine finds in Paul an apostle who is exquisitely sensitive to inner moral struggle. Perhaps he invents the Paul he finds. This is a landmark essay.]

## Trinity

Augustine. *The Trinity*. Trans. Edmund Hill, O. P. Brooklyn: New City Press, 1991. [Hill's introduction to Augustine's massively complex text is a marvel of concision and insight. The notes are very helpful too.]

Ayres, Lewis. *Nicaea and its Legacy: An Approach to Fourth-Century Trinitarian Theology*. New York: Oxford University Press, 2004. [The chapter on Augustine, an analysis of the "grammar" of his theology, illuminates both the spirit and the letter of his Trinitarian thinking.]

Stark, Judith Chelius. "Augustine on Women: Made in God's Image, But Less So." In *Feminist Interpretations of Augustine*. Ed. Stark. University Park, PA: The Pennsylvania State University Press, 2007, pp. 215–241. [Stark situates Augustine's notorious passage in *The Trinity* about women and the image of God (*Trin.* 12.7.10)—they bear the image, but not qua women—within the broader argument of books 12–15; she nurtures the hope that Augustine's Trinitarian appreciation for diversity within unity offers an alternative to his exclusion of women's bodies from divinity.]

TeSelle, Eugene. "Serpent, Eve, and Adam: Augustine and the Exegetical Tradition." In *Augustine: Presbyter Factus Sum*. Ed. Joseph T. Lienhard, Earl C. Miller, and Roland J. Teske. New York: Peter Lang, 1993, pp. 341–361. [This essay includes a nuanced discussion of book 12 of *The Trinity*, where Augustine "sets for himself the complex task of speaking both about what is *inwardly shared* by males and females and about what *inwardly and outwardly differentiates* them."]

## Use and enjoyment

O'Donovan, Oliver. "*Usus* and *Fruitio* in Augustine, *De Doctrina Christiana* I." *Journal of Theological Studies* 33.2 (1982) 361–397. [O'Donovan downplays the importance to Augustine of the distinction between use and enjoyment. It is a thought experiment that he soon abandons.]

Gregory, Eric. *Politics and the Order of Love: An Augustinian Ethic of Democratic Citizenship*. Chicago: University of Chicago Press, 2008. [Among its other virtues, this book contains the best recent discussion in the literature of Augustine's controversial distinction between use and enjoyment. See chapter 6, especially pp. 335–350. Gregory's animating concern: "How might the Augustinian tradition reconcile *love for neighbor with the love of God*?"]

## The inner teacher

Burnyeat, Miles. "Wittgenstein and Augustine *De magistro*." *Proceedings of the Aristotelian Society*. Supplementary Volume 61 (1987) 1–24; reprinted in *The Augustinian Tradition*. Ed. Gareth B. Matthews. Berkeley: University of California Press, 1999. [An influential attempt to divorce Augustine's reflections on teaching, sign language, and inner eye-witness from their theological context.]

Madec, Goulven, "*De magistro*: Langage et connaissance." In *Saint Augustin et la philosophie: Notes critiques*. Paris: Études Augustiniennes, 1996, pp. 53–60. [Madec, here and elsewhere, fights the good fight against atheological readings of Augustine's philosophy.]

## ALMOST AN EPILOGUE

### Augustine and Virgil

MacCormick, Sabine. *The Shadows of Poetry: Vergil in the Mind of Augustine*. Berkeley: University of California Press, 1998. [Virgil is still a frontier in Augustinian Studies, where Plotinus and Cicero are given pride of place. This is a pioneering work.]

# SUGGESTED READINGS, CHAPTER BY CHAPTER

## Donatism and religious coercion

Bowlin, John. "Augustine on Justifying Coercion." *Annual of the Society of Christian Ethics* 17 (1997) 49–70. [Without trying to justify Augustine's justification of coercion, Bowlin concocts the right tonic for overly self-confident liberal indignation. Stay tuned for his new book, *On Tolerance and Forbearance: Moral Inquiries Natural and Supernatural.*]

Kaufman, Peter Iver. *Incorrectly Political: Augustine and Thomas More.* Notre Dame: University of Notre Dame Press, 2007. [A meditation on the imperfection of all politics. Kaufman shows us how to be indebted to Augustine without having to be his apologist.]

Markus, R. A. *Saeculum: History and Society in the Theology of Saint Augustine.* Revised Edition. Cambridge: University of Cambridge Press, 1970. [The most influential study in the literature on the co-mingling of Augustine's two cities. The chapter on coercion, "*Coge Intrare*: The Church and Political Power," attempts to account for why Augustine missed the issue of the separation of powers, Church versus State (p. 149): "The reason why it did not occur to Augustine to restrict the scope of the state's proper sphere of action when he was thinking about religious coercion is simple: it did not occur to him to think in terms of the 'state' at all in this context."]

O'Donnell, James. *Augustine: A New Biography.* New York: HarperCollins, 2005. [The chapter on Donatism, entitled "The Augustinian Putsch in Africa," is both highly unsympathetic to Augustine and utterly riveting.]

## The political Augustine

Dodaro, Robert. *Christ and the Just Society in the Thought of Augustine.* Cambridge: Cambridge University Press, 2004. [Dodaro refuses, quite rightly, to remove the theology from the political thought, to remove Christ from the theology.]

Gregory, Eric. *Politics and the Order of Love: An Augustinian Ethic of Democratic Citizenship.* Chicago: University of Chicago Press, 2008. [Gregory refracts three varieties of modern liberalism—realist, proceduralist, civic—through the lens of Augustinian theology and discovers the lineaments of a politics of love. His aim is not to liberalize Augustine but to use Augustine's inspiration to deepen the political debate over the nature and future of liberalism.]

Kraynak, Robert P. *Christian Faith and Modern Democracy: God and Politics in the Fallen World.* Notre Dame: University of Notre Dame Press, 2001. [Kraynak argues that the tension between Augustine's two cities is as modern as it is ancient. He uses the Augustinian framework to critique the notion—a modern fiction, he thinks—that politics takes place on neutral ground, where certain inalienable human rights have to be assumed.]

Wolin, Sheldon. *Politics and Vision: Continuity and Innovation in Western Political Thought.* Expanded Edition. Princeton: Princeton University Press, 2004. [See Chapter Four, Sections IV to VII. Wolin finds in Augustine a depoliticized conception of time and a disposition to emphasize sociality over political power (p. 117): "The superiority of the social over the 'political' was a fundamental position in Augustine's thought."]

## Neo-paganism and its Augustinian animus

Connolly, William E. *Identity/Difference: Democratic Negotiations of Political Paradox*. Expanded Edition. Minneapolis: University of Minnesota Press, 1991. [Connolly is a political theorist of postmodern proclivities, and Augustine is the enemy that he loves the most. His "Letter to Augustine" (pp. 123–157) is not to be missed.]

Gay, Peter. *The Enlightenment: The Rise of Modern Paganism*. New York: W. W. Norton & Co., 1966. [It wasn't just about the triumph of science over superstition. The Enlightenment was a revival of classical sensibilities, more Roman than Greek, more pagan than Christian. This is the book to read to begin to get an understanding of the modernity that Augustine did not inspire.]

Milbank, John. *Theology and Social Theory: Beyond Secular Reason*. Second Edition. Oxford: Blackwell, 2006. [Milbank appropriates Augustine's critique of pagan virtue and turns it into a means to define a Christian postmodernism. No other kind is going to be especially plausible or palatable to him. See especially Milbank's last chapter, "The Other City: Theology as a Social Science."]

# GENERAL SUGGESTIONS FOR FURTHER READING

## BIOGRAPHIES

Brown, Peter. *Augustine of Hippo: A Biography.* A New Edition with an Epilogue. Berkeley: University of California Press, 2000. [This book is more than a biography. We get both the inner life of an extraordinary man and an insider's view to a time period—late antiquity—that emerges with its own claim to uniqueness. It hard to say whose genius is most in evidence here, Augustine or Brown's. The book is such a good read it is even harder to care about the difference.]

Chadwick, Henry. *Augustine: A Very Short Introduction.* Oxford: Oxford University Press, 1986. [More a history of Augustine's mind than his life, but still broadly biographical and interspersed with illustrations. As the title suggests, Chadwick's book is not long. His erudition is nevertheless evident throughout.]

O'Donnell, James J. *Augustine: A New Biography.* New York: HarperCollins, 2005. [This is more or less the unauthorized biography of Augustine. It emphasizes Augustine's extraordinary ability to manipulate his self-image, helped along by the naïveté of his readers. O'Donnell's achievement—and it is considerable—continues to ruffle the feathers of many an Augustine scholar. I confess that for me his book was a guilty pleasure.]

Wills, Garry. *Saint Augustine.* New York: Viking Penguin, 1999. [Wills brings a lively literary style to his classical erudition. He is especially good at getting the goods on Augustine's affective life (p. xx): "I shall be arguing, for instance, that he tells us far more about his mistress, and about the son they conceived and raised, than earlier biographers have recognized."]

## PHILOSOPHICALLY MINDED SURVEYS

Burnell, Peter. *The Augustinian Person.* Washington, D. C.: Catholic University Press, 2005. [A careful look at Augustine through the lens of "the great thesis" (p. 195): that "ultimately the various human modes of unity resolve into one," that "all reality has a sole, supreme principle."]

Matthews, Gareth B. *Augustine.* Oxford, Blackwell, 2005. [For an analytic treatment of discretely philosophical topics in Augustine, this book is an excellent choice. A few of the offerings: the Augustinian cogito, mind–body dualism, time and creation, the problem of evil.]

Rist, John. *Augustine: Ancient Thought Baptized.* Cambridge: Cambridge University Press, 1994. [Rist writes (p. 1): "Our subject, under its broadest description, is the Christianization of ancient philosophy in the version which was to be the most powerful and the most comprehensive." For philosophically engaging history of philosophy, this book has few rivals; none in Augustinian Studies.]

## THEOLOGICALLY MINDED SURVEYS

Burnaby, John. *Amor Dei: A Study of the Religion of St. Augustine.* Eugene, Oregon: Wipf & Stock, 1835. [Burnaby contests Anders Nygren's influential thesis that Augustine was too enamored of Platonic eros to have grasped Christian agape. More than that, his study is its own meditation on divine love, with Augustine as guide.]

Harrison, Carol. *Augustine: Christian Truth and Fractured Humanity.* Oxford: Oxford University Press, 2000. [A beautifully crafted amalgam of theological reflection and contextual analysis. From the forward (p. xii): "The first three chapters examine the philosophical, literary, and ethical aspects of Augustine's cultural context; the last three chapters consider the social context for Augustine's reflections upon the Church, forms of Christian life in the world and the nature of the two cities."]

TeSelle, Eugene. *Augustine the Theologian.* New York: Herder and Herder, 1970. [A comprehensive account of Augustine's theological development. TeSelle sorts out the constants from the variables very deftly (p. 347): "The unity of his thought is not the conceptual unity of a single system but the coherence of a single life animated by a passion for the truth and open to whatever might be learned about the one God and the one complex cosmos over which he rules."]

## ESSAY COLLECTIONS

Battenhouse, Roy W., ed. *A Companion to the Study of St. Augustine.* New York: Oxford University Press, 1955. [An old collection, but one that has worn surprisingly well. It is a good source for getting a sense of the Protestant appropriation of Augustine. Part Two is a critical guide to Augustine's major works.]

Dodaro, Robert and Lawless, George, ed. *Augustine and his Critics.* New York: Routledge, 2000. [Augustine has inspired controversy, both ancient and new. These essays take up the major bones of contention and assess whether he still has a leg or two to stand on. Sometimes Augustine comes off looking stronger, sometimes not.]

Matthews, Gareth B., ed. *The Augustinian Tradition.* Berkeley: University of California Press, 1999. [This eclectic collection gives evidence of Augustine's capacity to inspire minds across a wide range of temperaments. Note, for instance, the contrast between Alvin Plantinga's offering and that of

Richard Eldridge: the difference between a clarion's call to Christian philosophy and a literary meditation on the soul's ambiguities.]

Paffenroth, Kim and Kennedy, Robert P., ed. *A Reader's Companion to Augustine's Confessions.* Louisville, KY: Westminster John Knox, 2003. [There is a separate essay on each of the thirteen books of the *Confessions.* Each essay takes its book to be the key to the whole.]

Stump, Eleonore and Kretzmann, Norman, ed. *The Cambridge Companion to Augustine.* Cambridge: Cambridge University Press, 2001. [A wide-ranging collection of essays, mostly analytic in approach. Some of the topics covered: free will, original sin, memory, predestination, biblical interpretation, time and creation, Augustinian ethics, Augustine's medieval and modern legacy. James O'Donnell, one of Augustine's best biographers, contributes the opening essay on Augustine's life and times.]

## ANTHOLOGIES

Atkins, E. M. and Dodaro, R. J., ed. *Augustine: Political Writings.* Cambridge: Cambridge University Press, 2001. [A portrait of Augustine's political wisdom, delivered through sermons and letters.]

Burleigh, J. H. S., ed. *Augustine: Early Writings.* Philadelphia: The Westminster Press, 1953. [An excellent selection of texts, ranging from Augustine's retreat at Cassiciacum to the first work of his episcopate. Burleigh follows Augustine's own suggestion that in his second response to Simplician, he began a new phase of his theology—the later one.]

Burnaby, John, ed. *Augustine: Later Writings.* Philadelphia: The Westminster Press, 1955. [Selections from *The Trinity*, abbreviated *Homilies on the First Letter of St. John*, the full text of the underappreciated anti-Pelagian treatise, *The Spirit and The Letter.* Burnaby (p. 14): "The selection has been made in order to provide examples of the finest works of Augustine, as speculative and mystical theologian, as *Doctor Gratiae*, and as preacher of Charity."]

Harmless, William, ed. *Augustine In His Own Words.* Washington, DC: Catholic University of America Press, 2010. [By far the best anthology that is currently available. The selections take in major works and controversies and put forward an Augustine of multiple personae: philosopher, exegete, bishop, theologian, and preacher. This is a comprehensive but not overburdened look at the sum of Augustine's career. Harmless is very adept at setting a context.]

## REFERENCE WORKS

Fitzgerald, Allan D., O. S. A., ed. *Augustine through the Ages: An Encylopedia.* Grand Rapids, MI.: Eerdmans, 1999. [The standard one-volume reference on Augustine and his legacy. The entries, nearly five hundred of them, are prefaced by tables of Augustine's works, their abbreviations (which I follow), their dating, Latin editions, English translations.]

**GENERAL SUGGESTIONS FOR FURTHER READING**

Mayer, Cornelius P., ed. *CAG 2: Corpus Augustinianum Gissense.* Second Edition. Basel: Schwabe, 2004. [Augustine's Latin texts on CD-ROM. The search engine is powerful and relatively easy to use. Includes an extensive bibliography.]

O'Donnell, James J., ed. *Augustine: Confessions.* 3 volumes. Text and Commentary. Oxford: Clarendon Press, 1992. [A monumental achievement. The first volume, the Latin text, is a refinement of the efforts of Skutella (1934) and Verheijen (1981). The subsequent two volumes of commentary illuminate Augustine's confessional use of scripture and scriptural language, follow connections to his other works, canvas modern scholarship, and contextualize the big issues of interpretation.]

# INDEX

Adam and Eve 14, 90, 99
  Adam's self-aggrandizement 90–1
  Adam's sin 86–7
  Augustine's reading of story of 9, 83–4
  Eve's sin 87, 94
  fall of 68
  Pelagian view 14, 16
  redemption of Adam 93
  woman's role in Adam's crisis 93
Adeodatus, son of Augustine 35, 99, 100, 103, 104, 110–11
*Aeneid* (Virgil) 30–1, 105–6, 113–16, 122–4
Alypius 103–4
Ambrose, St. 103
angels
  fall of 91–2
Antiochus of Ascalon 20
Antony, Saint 103
asceticism
  Stoic and Manichean 27–8
*Attic Nights* (Aulus Gellius) 28–9
Atticus 17, 18
Augustine, Saint
  adolescent law-breaking 38–40
  association with Faustus 23–4
  baptism 103–4
  break from Manicheism 22–5
  coercive practices 119–22
  conversion 95–104
  critique of Platonists 49–50
  disagreement with Pelagians 13–14
  historical placement 1–3
  influence of Cicero 21–2, 23
  influence of his mother 42
  influence of Platonists 48–9, 55
  influence on Petrarch 70
  moment of illumination 103, 107
  narcissistic self-portraiture 30–7
  philosophical credentials 3–6
  sexual partner/partnership 99–100, 102
  turn to Paul 66–8, 82–3
  vision at Ostia 43
Augustine scholarship 10
Augustinians
  and philosophical inquiry 4–6

beauty 57, 58
  Augustine's recollection of 60–2
  God and 64–6
  Platonist 64
belief 117–18
body 64
  soul's descent into body 79–82
  soul without body 77–8

Caecilian 118
Caelestius 13–14
celibacy
  Augustine's embrace of 95–104, 106
Christianity
  Platonism and 50–2
  schism within North Africa 118–19
church
  Augustine's notion 7–8
Cicero 12, 13
  critique of Stoics 27–8
  on emotions 18–19
  on grief 17–21, 26, 28
  influence on Augustine 21–2, 23
  withdrawal from public life 17–18

# INDEX

*City of God* (Augustine) 14, 18, 28, 32, 63, 91, 116–17
*Confessions* (Augustine) 11, 13, 21–2, 26, 30–1, 32, 38, 41, 44, 51, 70, 73, 95, 100
*Consolatio* (Cicero) 18
continence 101–3
corruptibility 57
cosmology
  Manicheism's view of 22

death
  of Christ 40–2
  as evil and a punishment 16
  virtue and 13–17, 20–1, 26
dematerialization of value 26
demons
  sin and 90–2
desire 18, 19
  sexual 98–9, 105, 106, 107
  for wisdom 49–50
distress 18, 30
  Peripatetic and Stoic debate on 19–20
  *see also* grief
Donatism 118–19
  declared a heresy 2
  suppression of 119–21
Donatus the Great 118
dualism
  Manichean 24–5

Eden, garden of 14–15, 84
  sex in 99
election, doctrine of 45, 85–6
emotions
  forms and objects of 18–19, 20–1
  Stoic view (via Cicero) 29, 31
empiricism 4–6
*The Ends of Things Good and Bad* (Cicero) 20
*Enneads* (Plotinus) 48, 58–60, 79–80
Esau 6
Eve *see* Adam and Eve
evil 48

fallen angels 91–2
Faustus of Milevis 23–4

Gellius, Aulus 28
Gibbon, Edward 117
*The Gift of Perseverance* (Augustine) 13
God
  absolute simplicity of 63–4, 65–6
  act of betrayal 121–2
  beauty and 64–6
  existence of 56–7
  human image of triune 87–90
  of Manichees 53
  of the Platonists 62–6
  soul's ascent to 81–2
  Trinitarian bond 109–10
grace 85–6, 118, 120, 122
  human will and 45–8
  play between sin and 25
  radicalization of 6–7, 9–10, 107
grief
  Augustine's 27–30, 43
  Augustine's theatrical 30–5, 37–8
  Christ's experience of 29–30
  Cicero's critique 17–21, 26, 28
  wisdom as cure for 18
guilt *see* inherited guilt

Honorius, Roman Emperor 2, 116
*Hortensius* (Cicero) 22–3, 24, 26
Hume, David 117

inherited guilt 83–4, 86, 94–5
inner conflict 11–13, 124–5

Jacob 6, 85
Jesus Christ 111–12
  betrayal of 121–2
  death of 40–2
  experience of humanity 29–30
  incarnation 50–1
  parable of a great dinner 119–20
  parenting and 104
  perfection 15
Judas Iscariot 121–2
Julian of Eclanum 14, 25, 98

knowledge
  of earthly and temporal things 88–9
  Eve's taste of 94

## INDEX

language learning *see The Teacher*
(Augustine)
Lazarus 29
life
   *vita* versus *corpus* 64
logos 105–11
loss
   virtue and 16–17, 19–21, 26, 28–30
Lucretius
   disassociation of death from loss 16
lust (*concupiscentia*)
   Augustine's struggle with 95–6, 98–101, 105
   Eve and 87
   mere sex and 105

Mani 22
Manicheism 16, 22–4
   asceticism and 27–8
   cosmology and 24–5
   grief and 27
   materialism and 53
   practice of dematerialization 26
Marcellinus 116
Marcus Aurelius, Roman Emperor
   disassociation of death from loss 16
marriage 97, 106
   Monnica's plans for Augustine's 99
materialism
   differentiation and 53–4
   Manichean 53
   Plotinus on 58
memory *see* mind
mind
   as inward theater 70
   as memory 71–5
Monnica, mother of Augustine 2, 42–3, 99, 101

narcissism
   Augustine's confession of 35–8
Nebridius 35
neighbour-love 79

*On Free Will* (Augustine) 44, 68
*On the Good of Marriage*
(Augustine) 106

Origen 92
original sin
   Augustine's conception 9, 25, 83–4
   Caelestius' rejection of 13–14
   gender roles and 87–8
   *see also* sin

paganism 117
parenting 104, 105
Patricius, father of Augustine 2
Paul, Saint 46, 102, 103, 121
   Augustine's Pauline turn 66–8, 82–3
   Augustine's reading of 62–3, 85, 87
Pelagianism 27
   acceptance of naturalness of death 16
   disdain of Augustine's doctrine of original sin 13–14
Pelagius 13
Peripatetic philosophy
   on distressful emotions 19–20
Petrarch 70
philosophical inquiry
   Augustine's view of 50
   Augustinian *vs.* empiricist 4–6
Plato 3, 48, 50
Platonism/Platonists 66
   Augustine's will-spirit connection and 48–51
   beauty and 64
   Christianity and 50–2
   God and 62–3
pleasure 105–6
Plotinus 13, 48, 55
   Augustine's divergence from 82–3
   on materialism 58
   on place of unlikeness 58–9
   on soul's descent into body 79–82
Porphyry 55
prodigal son, parable of 38, 46–7, 51
   Augustine's version 38–9

reason 72–3
*regio dissimilitudinis see* unlikeness, place of
*Reconsiderations* (Augustine) 25
Rogatism 119

## INDEX

Satan 92
Saul 85–6
self
  Augustinian conception 11–12
  higher and lower selves 77–9
self-awareness 72
  insights of 61–2
self-definition
  importance of virtue to 15, 28–9
  loss of someone and 35–7
self-discipline 13–14
selfishness 87
  self in 78
self-presence 72–5
sensed world 4
  Platonists' distinction between sinful world and 48–51
sexual desire 98–9, 100, 105, 106, 107
simplicity 63–4, 65–6
sin
  appeal of sin itself 105
  Augustine's account of 38–9, 44–5
  Augustine's hesitations about willfulness of 39–40
  demons and 90–2
  grief over 30, 34–5
  motive of 83, 86
  penalty of 68–9, 84
  play between grace and 7–8, 10, 25
  as preference for temporal over eternal goods 44–5
  procreation and 9, 94–5
  responsibility for 9
  will to 44–7, 68–9
  *see also* inherited guilt; original sin
Socrates 3, 50
*Soliloquies* (Augustine) 72, 73, 97
soul/spirit
  All-Soul 80
  ascent to God 81–2
  descent into body 79–82
  divine inheritance 46–7
  place of unlikeness and 55–60
  prodigality and 39–40

  self-willed corruption and 84–5
  will and 48–51
*The Soul's Immortality* (Augustine) 73
Stoicism 27, 29, 49
  asceticism of 27–8
  theory of emotions 29, 31
  practice of dematerialization 26
  on preferable items 20

temptation 52, 56
theater
  Augustine and 30–5, 37–8
Theodosius I, Roman Emperor 2
*The Teacher* (Augustine)
  and language-learning 108–11
time 70–6, 125
*The Trinity* (Augustine) 87–8, 90
truth
  Augustine's engagement with 6–7, 24
Tullia, Cicero's daughter 17, 20
*Tusculan Disputations* (Cicero) 18
*Two Souls* (Augustine) 24–5

unlikeness, place of 55–60

vice
  struggle between virtue and 13–14, 25
victory
  a deflationary image (Virgil's) 105–6
Vincent, Rogatist bishop of Cartenna 119, 121
Virgil 13, 30–1, 105–6, 116, 117, 124
virtue
  Augustine's disagreement with Pelagians on 13–16
  centrality of 13
  divine favor and 45–6
  losable goods and 16–17, 19–21, 26, 28
Volusianus, proconsul of Africa 116

weakness
  Christ's kind of 66–9
will 107
  absoluteness of 44, 48

# INDEX

differentiated 54
sin and 44–7, 68–9, 105–6
spirit and 48–51
wisdom
   Christ as divine name for 23
   as cure for grief 18
   desire for infinite wisdom 49–50
   selfhood and 27

woman
   Augustine's figuration of 87–9
   being born of woman 97–8
   image of Trinity and 94
   role in Adam's crisis 93
Word made flesh 51
world
   sensed versus intelligible 48–51

# INDEX OF BIBLICAL REFERENCES

**Acts**
9:1–19   86

**Exodus**
3:14   56

**First Corinthians**
4:7   46
7:8–9   97
11:7   88–9

**First Timothy**
2:14   87

**Genesis**
1:26   88
1:27   88
2:7   97
2:17   87, 90–1
2:18   90, 101
2:21   93
2:22   90, 93
2:23   93
3:6   39, 86, 87
3:7   93
3:12   91
3:20   94
3:24   84

**John**
4:18   29
6:33   41
11:38   29

**Luke**
14:1   120
14:15–24   119
14:23   119
14:24   120
15:11–32   38
15:31–32   47

**Matthew**
8:8   11–12
19:21   103
26:38   29

**Psalms**
18:6   41

**Romans**
1:20   55, 57
8:32   121
9   6, 85, 107
13:13   51, 52, 105
13:14   51, 95, 104
14:1   103–4

www.ingramcontent.com/pod-product-compliance
Lightning Source LLC
Chambersburg PA
CBHW070333230426
43663CB00011B/2298